Essay Writing

Leaving Certificate Higher Level

PAULINE KELLY

FOLENS

Preface

How do we help students to bridge that gap between creative writing at Junior Level and the far more demanding task of writing a Leaving Certificate Essay?

Some students do not come to grips with the essay at any stage and they blunder along, never writing with confidence and certainly never enjoying the experience. The resultant writing is stilted and artificial, lacking that personal element which brings an essay to life and makes it a joy to read.

We must offer students a step-by-step approach, beginning with sentences and paragraphs and leading them on to planning and writing full essays. We must also help them to identify the kinds of essays which they enjoy writing and they can only find this out by lots of practice. Students will not write well in the exam if they have not been developing their writing potential throughout the senior cycle. This book at Higher Level and its companion volume at Lower Level aim to give students the practice and confidence they require in a guided approach to senior essays.

Somewhere along the way, our students should make the happy discovery that,
"You write because you've got something to say."
F. Scott Fitzgerald.

Pauline Kelly.

Acknowledgements

Folens would like to thank the following for their permission to reproduce extracts. Combat Poverty Agency for extract "Women & Poverty in Ireland" by Mary Daly; Irish Independent for "Jailed Soccer Thugs Freed;" Collins Publishers for "Inside Russia Today" by Alan Moorehead; David Higham Associates Ltd. for "Let Sleeping Vets Lie" by James Herriot; Maeve Binchy and The Irish Times for "Children on Holiday" first published in the Irish Times on October 30th 1974.

While considerable effort has been made to locate all holders of copyright material used in this text, we have failed to contact some of these. Should they wish to contact Folens Publishers, we would be glad to come to some arrangement with them.

***Editor*:** Antoinette Higgins

Artwork: Mary Murphy

Cover Design*:* Phillip Ryan

Page Make-up and Design: Teresa Burke

Output at Type Bureau

Produced by Folens

ISBN: 0 86121 0115

© — **Folens Publishing Company** 1990

All rights reserved. No part of this publication may be reproduced or transmitted in any form or by any means (stencilling, photocopying, etc.) for whatever purpose, even purely educational without written permission from the publisher.

The publisher reserves the right to change, without notice at any time, the specification of this product, whether by change of materials, colours, bindings, format, text revision or any other characteristic.

Contents

The Purpose of This Book 4

Examination Essays since 1977 6

Stage 1 — The Sentence 9

Stage 2 — Types of Essays 19

Stage 3 — Paragraphs .26

Stage 4 — Planning a Full Essay 60

Stage 5 — Writing a Full Essay 75

The Purpose of This Book

The essay carries a very substantial percentage of the total marks awarded at Leaving Certificate Higher Level — more than any other single question. Failure to achieve a good honours grade overall is most often the result of a poorly written essay.

In the past 10 years, examiners have repeatedly made the following criticisms:

- Many candidates make a bad choice and write a shallow, uninteresting essay, never really coming to grips with the subject undertaken.

- Candidates do not know how to *start* their essay.

- Candidates do not know how to *organise* and *paragraph* their work.

- Candidates do not know how to successfully *conclude* their essay.

This book deals with all 4 of these factors and aims to give lots of writing practice to students who want to develop good writing ability.

H.L. Essay Writing

Essays at Leaving Certificate level demand more of your imagination and intellect than those you wrote at junior level. On first looking at exam papers you may feel very dismayed and wonder how on earth you can possibly write several pages of foolscap on any of the following topics.

(a) Life is a sequence of surprises.
(b) Nature's disregard for man.
(c) The importance of music in your life.
(d) Gossip.
(e) Just after sunrise.
(f) What it means to be Irish.
(g) The take-away.
(h) This great stage of fools.

(1989 Higher Level — Paper I)

(a) Memories.
(b) The teenage cultural scene.
(c) Man's inventive mind — his glory or his doom?
(d) What future for the "Third World?"
(e) An open letter to the Minister for Education.
(f) Is it time for male liberation?
(g) What place for literature in the television age?
(h) Violence in everyday life.

(1986 Higher Level — Paper I)

The 5 stages in this book are designed to draw out your potential for writing good, interesting essays. If you work at it, stage by stage, you may surprise yourself with your ability to write. Somewhere along the way, you should discover a style of writing that is personal to you and that you enjoy. Good essay writing is not just filling the page with the required number of words or writing grimly until you have filled a page or two of foolscap. You should write beause you want to communicate *your* thoughts or *your* experiences. If you begin to see it that way, you will write much better than if you see it as a dull chore.

"Writing comes more easily if you have something to say."

Sholem Asch

H.L. Essay Writing

Essays set on Leaving Certificate Higher Course Papers since 1977

(a) Man as victim and master of his environment.
(b) The sweet security of streets.
(c) Nothing venture, nothing win.
(d) Science without conscience is the ruin of a people.
(e) The artist and society.
(f) A good book is the best of friends.
(g) The world does not progress; it merely changes.
(h) Physical fitness.

(1977)

(a) Roads.
(b) My attitude to pop music.
(c) "The age of chivalry is dead."
(d) Are young people happier today than they were a hundred years ago?
(e) Why you would, or would not, like to be a world leader.
(f) Why read poetry?
(g) The ideal companion.
(h) Ireland is still the best country in which to live.

(1978)

(a) Every man for himself.
(b) Magic.
(c) What every parent should know.
(d) "Music is the greatest of the arts." What do you think?
(e) Happiness: a good bank account, a good cook, and a good digestion.
(f) Is science the enemy of poetry?
(g) The role of women in Ireland today.
(h) The preservation of wild life.

(1979)

(a) Dreams.
(b) The lessons of history.
(c) The energy crisis.
(d) Life begins at twenty.
(e) Violence in sport.
(f) The future of religion.
(g) The lure of the countryside.
(h) You have been asked to contribute an article to a serious journal on your favourite poet, or dramatist or novelist. Write out the article you would submit.

(1980)

H.L. Essay Writing

(a) This wonderful world.
(b) Festivals — are they really worth while?
(c) Digging up the past.
(d) Journeys.
(e) How to deal with the young offender.
(f) Harvesting the seas.
(g) No person is completely free.
(h) Literature is simply a form of escape.

(1981)

(a) Castles in the air.
(b) The computer — a friend or enemy of man?
(c) Modern Ireland — a country for the young?
(d) Education for leisure.
(f) Should Ireland develop nuclear energy?
(g) Springtime.
(h) Pop music reflects the interests of its time.

(1982)

(a) The young — slaves of fads and fashions.
(b) Pests.
(c) The unemployment problem.
(d) Falling in love.
(e) The value of the visual arts.
(f) "Men learn little from the experience of others."
(g) Your view of women's liberation.
(h) Preserving our heritage is a luxury we cannot afford.

(1983)

(a) Silence.
(b) Youth is wasted on the young.
(c) "Romantic Ireland's dead and gone."
(d) The cosmetics industry — boon or fraud.
(e) Is it right to experiment with animals?
(f) Boys and girls should get the same kind of education.
(g) "Tis a mad world, my masters."
(h) The joy of reading.

(1984)

(a) My kind of music.
(b) Reafforestation.
(c) "Science fiction" — fact or fiction?
(d) Drug abuse.
(e) Window-dressing — a symbol of our age.
(f) International sport.
(g) The opposite sex.
(h) Robots, human and mechanical.

(1985)

H.L. Essay Writing

(a) Memories.
(b) The teenage cultural scene.
(c) Man's inventive mind — his glory or his doom?
(d) What future for the "Third World?"
(e) An open letter to the Minister for Education.
(f) Is it time for male liberation?
(g) What place for literature in the television age?
(h) Violence in everyday life.
(1986)

(a) Killing time.
(b) Art in everyday life.
(c) A sense of humour.
(d) The scientific or technological development of recent years which is likely to have most impact on mankind.
(e) Raindrops.
(f) Man's inhumanity to man.
(g) Bores.
(h) Write out a sermon you would like to deliver to a full congregation in Church or a speech you would like to make in Dáil Eireann.
(1987)

(a) The ambitions I hope to have realised by the age of thirty.
(b) After the holocaust.
(c) Sounds in the night.
(d) What Ireland needs is self-sacrifice and hard work.
(e) "What should a man do but be merry?"
(f) "School has failed us." Do you agree?
(g) Do newspapers serve a useful purpose?
(h) Horrors of the modern city.
(1988)

(a) Life is a sequence of surprises.
(b) Nature's disregard for man.
(c) The importance of music in your life.
(d) Gossip.
(e) Just after sunrise.
(f) What it means to be Irish.
(g) The take-away.
(h) This great stage of fools.
(1989)

(a) Breaking barriers.
(b) The importance of drama.
(c) My ideal magazine.
(d) Write the speech which you would make for or against the motion: "That Ireland cherishes all her young people equally."
(e) Modern snobbery.
(f) The minor pleasures of my life.
(g) "To make us love our country, our country ought to be lovely."
(h) Hairstyles.
(1990)

STAGE 1

The Sentence

The sentence is the basic building brick of all good writing. Many essays are ruined because of lack of attention to the basic rules of written English. Originality and creativity are wonderful assets in the area of ideas but spelling and punctuation must never be forgotten even when the writing is inspired!

Here are some sentences in which the writers have totally neglected the basic rules. Rewrite each sentence, *marking capital letters and all punctuation marks in red.*

christmas the season of goodwill happiness and gluttony has always filled me with dread

for some computers are the perfect answer to tedious work for others they represent redundancy

rubbish cried the maths teacher thats no way to go about this problem

hamlet by william shakespeare is one of the worlds best known plays

can reading really improve my basic writing skills

ten swansea soccer fans were released from a prison at khalkis 55 miles north of athens

i read the irish times on saturday morning and my father reads the press

french airline officials have said that a dc 10 carrying 73 dutch businessmen crashed over the sahara desert yesterday

H.L. Essay Writing

Bear in Mind the Following Points

- Keep your sentences at a reasonable length. Long, rambling, confused sentences are disastrous.

- Simplicity is better than long-winded ranting. Know what you want to say in a sentence and say it clearly.

- Vary the length of your sentences but always bear in mind that none should be too long.

- It is a very good test of your work to read it aloud. The standard of essay writing would rise immediately if more candidates did this simple test when writing essays throughout their senior cycle.

- The examiner who reads your Leaving Certificate essay is trying to assess the quality of your work. If you observe the basic rules of good, written English, your ideas will come across clearly. If you do not observe these rules, your message becomes garbled and difficult to read and understand.

→ Reasonable Length.
→ SIMPLICITY
→ VARY LENGTH
→ Read aloud.
→ Good English.

H.L. Essay Writing

To illustrate this last point, let's look at two examples of writing. On the left, we see a carelessly written passage. On the right, the same piece of writing, but here the rules have been observed and the ideas are therefore easy to read and understand. Read them both and imagine your reaction if you were the examiner.

The Pleasures of Reading

My best friends have always been books I still have an old and very copy of cinderella bought for me in waterstones when I was just 2 years old im told i grabbed it from a shelf and sank my teeth in it so it had to be purchased. all the stages of my life have being marked by different characters writers and book titles there was noddy Roald Dahl betsy Byars Judy blume Watership down and then the hobbit For while i went through a dungeons and dragons phase I can still hear my mother shouting up to my room on sunny days put down that book and go outside. Last year I read 20 best sellers the kind you buy at airports railway stations. I even started writing one until i found it was lot harder than it looked have you every tried writing a novel about industrial espionage set in the suburbs of beirut it could fill in a afternoon for you some day.

The Pleasures of Reading

My best friends have always been books. I still have an old and very tattered copy of "Cinderella," bought for me in "Waterstone's" when I was just 2 years old. I'm told I grabbed it from a shelf and sank my teeth in it, so it had to be purchased.

All the stages of my life have been marked by different characters, writers and book titles. There was "Noddy", Roald Dahl, Betsy Byars, Judy Blume, "Watership Down" and then "The Hobbit." For a while, I went through a "Dungeons and Dragons" phase. I can still hear my mother shouting up to my room on sunny days, "put down that book and go outside!"

Last year, I read 20 best sellers, the kind you buy at airports and railway stations. I even started writing one until I found it was a lot harder than it looked. Have you ever tried writing a novel about industrial espionage, set in the suburbs of Beirut? It could fill in a wet afternoon for you some day!

Essay Writing

Now rewrite the following passage correctly:

The dog — friend or enemy of man?

Is the dog really mans best friend that snarling growling toothy creature in your neighbours garden could only be seen as the enemy of civilized human beings. Isnt he the one who fouled the footpath just at the point where you stepped out of the car last sunday isnt he the one who howled loudly until 2 am the night before your christmas exams and did he have anything to do with the missing 5 pounds of sausages the day of the barbecue last summer

Expanding Your Vocabulary

"I'm speaking from the cossack," he said in a subdued shout.
"From the what?"
The cossack, the telephone cossack in t'village."
"Yes, indeed," I said, "and what can I do for you?"
"I want you to come out as soon as possible, to treat a calf for semolina."
"I beg your pardon?"
"I 'ave a calf with semolina."
"Semolina?"
"Aye, that's right. A feller was on about it on t'wireless the other morning."
"Oh! Ah yes, I see." I too had heard a bit of the farming talk on Salmonella infection in calves.

"He said you could send samples off to the labrador," said Mr. Pickersgill.
"Eh? To the what?"
"The investigation labrador — you know."
"Oh yes, quite, but I don't think that the lab would be of any help in this case."

James Herriot
Let Sleeping Dogs Lie

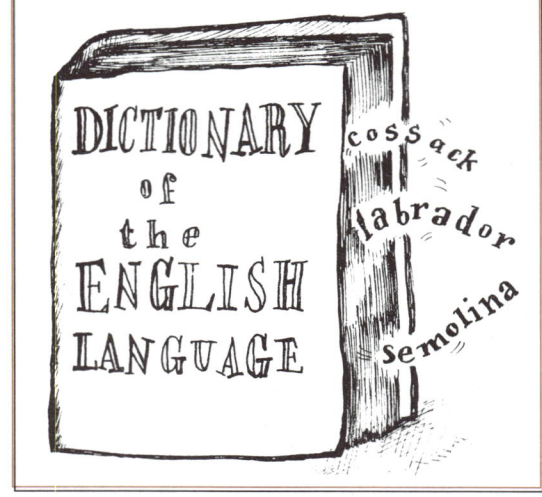

Mr. Pickersgill obviously had a problem with words. This is very comical in print. But it is not really funny to go through life mispronouncing words just because you have never developed a good vocabulary.

You should never use long words just for the sake of it, but neither should your conversation be handicapped by a lack of vocabulary.

H.L. Essay Writing

The words and phrases in italics below are either awkward or inexact. Replace them with the better chosen words from the column on the right.

1. The door opened *without our pushing it*.
2. Our new neighbours are more *rich* than we are.
3. The *person who told the story* was not involved in it.
4. High-rise office blocks were a new *thing* in the Dublin of the sixties.
5. The *people in charge* denied that there had been a riot.
6. The nuclear bomb *damaged* Hiroshima.
7. Stephen King writes *weird* novels.
8. There was *sly dealing* in the recent government elections.
9. I'm looking for a *fancy* holiday destination.
10. Their prices *went lower than* their competitors.
11. There was a lot of *trouble* in the newspapers about the athletes' proposed tour.
12. They picked their way through the *stones and bits of wood* after the bombing.

8. corruption
12. rubble
10. undercut
1. automatically
3. narrator
7. affluent
11. controversy
4. phenomenon
2. sinister
5. authorities
6. devastated
9. exotic

Listen to people talking around you. Most people use a very restricted vocabulary. You can do better if you work at it. Read good fiction and good newspapers. An examiner wants to see that you have a good command of the English language. What efforts do you make to improve your standards? Having and *making use of* a good dictionary is a start.

13

H.L. Essay Writing

Rewrite the following sentences, using the words on the right to fill the gaps.

1. The protesters held placards — the need for radical reform.
2. According to some — the border guards fired without warning.
3. The unstable country was further hit by a mass — of academics, doctors and skilled workers.
4. The minister announced new — to deal with current financial problems.
5. Talks to — the long-running dispute broke down in the early hours of this morning.
6. There is — in government circles about the implications of recent decisions in the High Court.
7. The first in a — of one-day strikes will begin on Monday of next week.
8. The accused man claimed that he had been threatened while in police — .
9. The violent storming of the embassy was the latest — in a week of riots in the capital.
10. Plans for a proposed nuclear plant have been — due to continued protests by residents.

4. strategies
10. scrapped
7. series
3. exodus
6. apprehension
8. custody
9. atrocity
1. proclaiming
5. resolve
2. eyewitnesses

H.L. Essay Writing

Rewrite the following 2 newspaper articles, filling in the gaps with the words on the right.

Minister Bans Product

A Hallowe'en novelty product of false skin, sold under the — name "Living Death" is — to health and was banned yesterday by the — for Industry and Commerce. Parents are — to be on the look-out and not to — it.
The product is a — latex which is sold — the country and contains enough ammonia to cause dizziness and possibly other — problems. Two young boys have already been — by the product and required medical — .

throughout	Minister
respiratory	brand
treatment	affected
warned	harmful
liquid	purchase
treatment	

Man found alive in highway wreckage

Californian rescue crews yesterday pulled a motorist alive from beneath the double-decker Oakland highway that collapsed in Tuesday's — earthquake. The 57-year-old man, named as Buck Helms, was — to hospital after being pulled from the — some 90 hours after the earthquake. The car was spotted on Friday night when engineers were testing the structural — by pulling on sections of the highway to see whether it was stable for — rescue work.
An engineer said that early yesterday he saw some movement in the car. The man was found nearly 12 hours after the rescue was called off because workers said the wreckage was unstable and — the searchers.
The — was one of 80 names that Oakland police had on a list of "missing — ". Initially, authorities speculated that as many as 250 people had been crushed in their — . The — is now about 55.
The danger of collapse was so well known that a popular bumper sticker in Oakland read, "Pray For Me, I Ride The Nimitz Freeway."

vehicles	further
rushed	survivor
endangered	toll
massive	wreckage
strength	persons

15

H.L. Essay Writing

Using the vocabulary on the right, complete the following sentences taken from newspaper articles:

1. Half the — from the Lottery will be devoted to prize money.
2. No — are expected, following the latest wave of violence.
3. The Minister said the idea was the — of a Cork businessman.
4. The government spokesman said they had lifted all — on free speech in the country.
5. The young man was charged with possession of a semi-automatic pistol with — to endanger life.
6. The Soviet leadership has gradually been — relations with the Orthodox Church.
7. Shop windows were smashed during a drunken — through the city.
8. After the crash, the authorities said they could not rule out — .
9. Temporary — was caused to traffic during the demonstration.
10. Trade Union — are meeting the Minister to discuss the issue today.

officials

sabotage

rampage

restoring

reprisals

brainchild

restrictions

revenue

intent

disruption

H.L. Essay Writing

The following passage is an extract from Max Caulfield's book "The Easter Rebellion". It describes how the looting began in shops near the G.P.O. on Easter Monday, 1916. Through careful choice of words and phrases and excellent sentence construction, this author writes a wonderful descriptive passage. The incidents happened almost 80 years ago but he makes the scene as vivid as an article from today's newspaper.

"Hooroosh! Hooroosh!" shouted the drunken old woman. "They're raiding Noblett's." And her shawl-covered arms flapped excitedly like two great black wings.

Up out of the slums, the worst in Europe at that time outside the stews of Naples, from the tenements of Gardiner Street and Marlborough Street, from the back streets behind Moore Street and Great Britain Street, swarmed the underprivileged — or as 1916 knew them, the poor. The women outnumbered the men by at least four to one. There were old crones in their black shawls and young girls in their bare feet. The men wore mufflers round their throats and even their caps were ragged and dirty. The backsides of urchins showed bare through their ragged pants and the little girls had grubby pinafores.

Suddenly, with a tremendous crash, the plate-glass front of Noblett's, a confectioner's on the corner of Sackville Street and North Earl Street, crashed on to the pavement.

Sweets spilled out in a cascade; and men, women and children dived to the ground to scoop up handfuls of chocolates, Turkish delight, glacier mints and fruit bon-bons. Glass jars stuffed wth sweetmeats were smashed and boxes ripped open and the contents strewn over the street. The mob grew wild with excitement and, as news of the spoils available spread, swelled in size. Then in the middle of all the looting, somebody shouted, "The soldiers are coming!"

There was a swift scattering. Women and children knocked and trampled each other down as they surged towards O'Connell Bridge. But when the military failed to appear, they crowded back to Noblett's again.

Once one shop had gone there was no halting the destruction. Quickly two others were broken into, the noise of their crashing plate glass sounding all the louder because of the new and awful stillness that had fallen over the city. Guttersnipes ran out of Dunn's, the hatters, decked out in silk hats, straw hats and bowlers. One urchin danced to the edge of the pavement with the three different varieties perched perilously on his head, on top of each other. A second made a swipe at him and knocked the lot over. As the hats landed in the gutter, his friends began to kick them about like footballs. Drunken women reeled from the Saxone shoe shop, brandishing satin slippers and knee-high Russian boots. It was like a gigantic lucky dip; and by the hazard of chance, too, some got too much of one article and not enough of another. Women, clasping boxes of shoes to their breasts, fought their way out of the shops, only to find that they had grabbed a whole series of left-foots. A barter system was soon established. "A lady's No. 4 black Russian boot with fur lining — left foot only," shouted a woman, hoping to find its companion.

Sean O'Casey watched a slum crowd fling clothing all over Sackville Street and try on brand-new garments over their rags; one woman got into the wrecked tram at the corner of North Earl Street and stripped to try on camisoles. A man ran past him carrying a jar of whiskey in one hand and a pair of looted boots in the other, and O'Casey saw a bullet hit the jar and smash it.

Pubs, of course were obvious targets. In Henry Street, women dragged a case of champagne into the street and danced around it, only desisting from time to time to drink the contents.

For James Connolly the looting posed an agonizing dilemma. The people committing it were the poor, the downtrodden and the ignorant — the very people to whom he had dedicated his life; the people who stood to benefit most if he won what he had set himself out to win. Yet they were not only disgracing the insurrection; they were hindering it. Sadly Connolly ordered, "Fire a volley over their heads."

H.L. Essay Writing

The first volley scattered the looters, but they quickly gathered again and a second volley had to be fired.

"Ah, they're only blanks!" shouted a man and led the way into another shop.

Max Caulfield

Features of Good Writing in the Passage Above

1. The use of sentences of varying length to give the narrative balance and variety. Sometimes, a paragraph begins with a short, dramatic sentence which sets the scene.
   Find 2 examples.

2. Some sentences create lively, colourful mental pictures as you read. These very vivid images enliven the narrative.
   Find 2 examples.

3. The use of dialogue to give a sense of drama to the narrative.
   Find 2 examples.

4. The careful choice of **verbs** to convey the excited atmosphere.
   Find 2 examples.

5. A rich vocabulary which shows itself in apt choice of words and phrases which make the whole scene very vivid and immediate for the reader.
   Find 2 examples.

STAGE 2
Examining the Types of Essays

There are basically 3 types of essays:
- Narrative
- Descriptive
- Discursive

Look back to the essay titles at the beginning of this book. Each year, there are 8 essays, giving you scope for different styles of writing.

The titles fall into 3 basic types named above (narrative, descriptive, discursive), but we can further categorise them as follows:

1. **Descriptive**
   Silence.
   Springtime.
   Journeys.
   The lure of the countryside.
   Raindrops.
   Sounds in the night.

Do you read novels to help develop your style?

(**N.B.** Any of the above might become titles of narrative essays).

Do you listen to political programmes on radio and television? Do you read quality newspapers/magazines? Do you take part in or attend school debates?

2. **Discursive**
   "School has failed us." Do you agree?
   Is it time for male liberation?
   Youth is wasted on the young.
   The future of religion.
   How to deal with the young offender.
   Man's inhumanity to man.
   Nature's disregard for man.
   This great stage of fools.
   The young — slaves of fads and fashion.

H.L. Essay Writing

3. **Environmental**
Reafforestation.
Harvesting the seas.
The energy crisis.
Man as victim and master of his environment.
Preserving our heritage is a luxury we cannot afford.

Do you read newspapers, letters to the editor, features pages?

Are you a regular visitor to your local library? Do you browse in bookshops? Do you enjoy music, painting?

4. **Literary and Artistic**
What place for literature in the modern age?
Science fiction — fact or fiction?
The joy of reading.
Literature is simply a form of escape.
An article for a journal on your favourite poet, dramatist, novelist.
A good book is the best of friends.
"Music is the greatest of the arts." What do you think?

5. **Personal**
The ambitions I hope to have realised by the age of thirty.
The importance of music in your life.
Why you would or would not like to be a world leader......or a politician in Dáil Eireann.

Do you keep a diary? ... write songs or poems?

Do you take part in school debates? Do you like listening to political discussion?

6. **Irish Interest**
Modern Ireland — a country for the young.
Romantic Ireland's dead and gone.
Should Ireland develop nuclear energy?
What Ireland needs is self-sacrifice and hard work.
What it means to be Irish.

H.L. Essay Writing

Look back to the following exam papers,
- 1981
- 1983
- 1988

and fit the essays into the categories above.

> **Important note before you begin!**
> Beware of too narrow an interpretation of any title. "Springtime" could be interpreted as an essay on youth. "Silence" could become a short story. "Journeys" is open to several interpretations, factual, descriptive or narrative. Time spent thinking about the possibilities of the title is valuable time.

Your aim is to find the type of essay you like to write and are good at.

Some Guidelines for Good Writing

It is important that you value *your own* feelings and experience and write from what you know. Most professional writers keep a notebook in which they constantly jot down their observations of life and people. This is a very good way to begin if you would like to publish your writing at some stage. Don't reject your own world and feelings, use them!

Examiners read hundreds of scripts and it is a delight to find an essay that is sincere and interesting. When we read, our excitement comes from those moments when we connect with the text in front of us, when we recognise something that the author has also noticed and has expressed for us. The good author writes as much from the heart as from the head, and you should aim to do the same.

Above all, do not be tempted to learn off prepared topics which you will drag in under any title in the exam. You will probably end up with an essay which is not relevant to the title and this is disastrous. If you practise writing a lot, you will gain confidence and begin to trust yourself and your ability. James Joyce said,
"Imagination is memory."
Think about that. If it was good enough for James Joyce…

H.L. Essay Writing

Here is a good example of a professional writer who is writing an interesting, imaginative article mainly from her personal memories:

Children on Holiday

Anyone who has ever taken children on an outing *en masse* knows that they don't remember the Norman castle, the Renaissance sculpture or the ancient spear, they think happily about the beans and chips in a cafe, the buying of souvenirs, the sending of funny postcards, and racing each other up and down the Hill of Tara. The culture is only the background for the day out. So before you invest great savings in giving a child an experience which will stand to him for a lifetime, it might be no harm to investigate other possibilities like one of those educational cruises which kids love, or sending them for a week to a distant cousin's farm or to learn sailing while you have your own holiday and no rows.

Of course, some parents really do try very hard, like a couple I know who rented a horse-drawn caravan just to please the children. They were successful at making the three kids happy but at a great cost to themselves. The first day out, the horse ate every flower in a cottage garden and they had to pay the owner and put up with a lot of abuse. The children decided the horse was hungry as a result and gave him fish fingers which burned his mouth and they had to take him to a vet in the next town. One day they tackled the wrong horse to the caravan by mistake and he went off like Nijinsky and they were pursued by the farmer who owned him and the police who had been alerted. Finally, on the last night, exhausted, they bought a bottle of gin and drank half of it to ease their miseries. Next morning they awoke to the news that the youngest child thought the horse needed a drink of water and had given him the rest of the gin. But they at least have the satisfaction of knowing that "it was the best holiday ever," which is more than a lot of parents can know.

When I was a child I always hoped that a holiday would mean a chance to outwit some dangerous criminals, and had visions of evil men with bags of loot saying: "Garn, imagine being caught by a young girl." It was very difficult to find gangs of villains in Ballybunion, but I would sit glowering at the big hotel, thinking that this was where they might operate from, and following innocent tourists up the road while taking notes to such extent that the manager once asked me was anything disturbing me? He would show me round the premises if I liked, and I rightly took it as the polite preliminary to being told to push off.

Like every child, I suppose I searched in vain for wrecked ships, and the odd pirate, and hoped that the daily bus from Listowel might bring in some secret agents who would recruit me because of my knowledge of the place. And again like any other child, the makeshift meals that we would eat the night we arrived when nothing was unpacked were more enjoyable and memorable by far than the normal ones which people had to go to trouble over.

So think carefully the next time you see a notice saying 'Reduced Price for Children.' They may love it all of course, and you are good and kind to bring them with you instead of packing them away to a camp like all Americans seem to do. But don't expect them to be grateful automatically. Children are much nicer than we are really, and they like to meet their own species and do something. It's not enough to say you have been there, they aren't old enough for that sort of thing yet.

From *Children on Holiday* by Maeve Binchy, published in *The Irish Times, 30 October 1974*.

1. Did you find yourself making "connections" with this text? At what points did you read something you recognised as part of your own experience?
2. How would you describe Maeve Binchy's style of writing?
3. Write 100 words (approx.) on your own most vivid memories of childhood outings or holidays.

H.L. Essay Writing

Interpretations

To illustrate the point that titles are open to varying interpretations let us take the 1987 essay "Killing Time."

The following passages are taken from essays written by Leaving Certificate students. The examples show that some students took the word "killing" as a verb, while others treated it as an adjective. The essays written reflect these differing interpretations.

Read the extracts and comment on the qualities of each.

A. Killing Time

The saying may be old, but it is not out of date; "time is of the essence." Today, almost everything has a definite time limit. We live by the clock, by the calendar, by the calculator. We work to deadlines and we kill each minute with digital precision ...

B. Killing Time

1975 — Cambodia. The nightmare begins. Pol Pot and his fanatical rebel army, the Khymer Rouge seize power. The people are forcibly moved from the cities to the land. Mass executions are commonplace. The sick, the wealthy, the intelligent, the troublesome, all are eliminated with ruthless efficiency. Killing time has come and a reign of terror grips the country ...

C. Killing Time

He was a busy man, Mr. Julian R. T. Prellis, a very busy man. He had discovered personal fulfillment in packing his waking hours with great volumes of paperwork. He often thought to himself how lucky he was to thrive on work. There were so many shirkers in his office who dodged at every opportunity. He never went home before 7 p.m. and he found holidays tiresome and pointless. It came as a great shock to Mr. Prellis when his firm "Gnome Clockmaking Co." announced redundancies and he was part of the first batch. The manager was sympathetic, it would only be a short time before the firm pulled through the bad patch. Until then, he would just have to kill time ...

D. Killing Time

The measurement of time has become increasingly important to us with the advance of civilisation. Once, time was based on the succession of night and day, the waxing and waning of the moon and the changing seasons of the year. Now, we live and work by ever more precisely measured time. What do we mean by "Killing Time"? If time is infinite, how can we kill it? It is strange to think that while I am passing time, someone else is wasting or killing it, while a third person is counting it and perhaps you are just living it. Now I know that Shakespeare expressed views on time far more eloquently than I can, but I have an hour to kill and you've got to take the time to read what I've written.

H.L. Essay Writing

E. Killing Time

"Lock 'em an' load 'em! the stealthy platoon commander whispered in a deep Mississippi accent. The men of "Bravo Company" slowly trudged their way out of their firebase. My hand slowly but steadily slammed the bolt on my automatic rifle into firing position. Only the moon, which was hidden intermittently behind a dark veil of cloud, illuminated the dirt trail before us. We knew this light would be of little use once we entered the jungle.

Everything about our platoon spelled out warning, for this troop was hardened, professional and looking for Vietnamese blood.

On previous encounters with the well equipped North Vietnamese Army we had been almost devastated, due to their sheer strength in numbers. But not now. We had, for long enough, taken everything that could be thrown at us. It was now our turn to inflict some real pain. It was now time to teach these people a lesson. It was now killing time.

F. Killing Time

This morning it had all seemed so easy, a phone call, cutting short his troubled dreams, the voice of his C.D. on the line.

"Karl, you awake son?"

"Yes sir, Colonel Anderson sir!"

"Get your men together, we're going to hit those V.C. so hard, they'll think war has been re-invented!"

"Yes sir!" At briefing, they were told it would be easy, a "mopping-up" operation. Karl knew differently the moment he saw the field. The foul stench of death hung in the air and there was no cover. They had no choice but to cross that terrible expanse. Karl spoke,

"I believe that field is mined sir..."

Write an opening paragraph for the essay **Killing Time.**

H.L. Essay Writing

Descriptive Writing

Nuclear Holocaust

There were missiles.
Under the earth.
In the sky.
Beneath the waves.
Missiles with thermo-nuclear warheads, enough to kill everybody on earth.
Three times over.
And something set them off; sent them flying, West to East and East to West crossing in the middle like cars on a cable railway.

East and West, the sirens wailed. VIPs went to their bunkers and volunteers stood at their posts. Suddenly, nobody wanted to be an engine-driver anymore, or a model or a rock-star. Everybody wanted to be one thing: a survivor. But it was an overcrowded profession.

The missiles climbed their trajectory arcs, rolled over the top and came down, accelerating. Below, everyone was ready. The Frimleys had their shelter in the lounge. The Bukovskys favoured the cellar...

Down came the missiles. Some had just the one warhead, others had several, ranging from the compact warhead to the large, family size. Every town was to receive its own, individually programmed warhead. Not one had been left out.

They struck, screaming in with pinpoint accuracy, bursting with blinding flashes, brighter than a thousand suns. Whole towns and city centres vaporized instantly; while tarmac, trees and houses thirty miles from the explosions burst into flames. Fireballs, expanding in a second to several miles across, melted and devoured all matter that fell within their diameters. Blast-waves, travelling faster than sound, ripped through the suburbs. Houses disintegrated and vanished. So fierce were the flames that they devoured all the oxygen around them, suffocating those people who had sought refuge in deep shelters. Winds of a hundred and fifty miles an hour, rushing in to fill the vacuum, created fire storms that howled through the streets, where temperatures in the thousands cooked the subterranean dead. The very earth heaved and shook as the warheads rained down, burst upon burst upon burst, and a terrible thunder rent the skies.

For an hour the warheads fell, then ceased. A great silence descended over the land. The Bukovskys had gone, and the Frimleys were no more. Through the silence, through the pall of smoke and dust that blackened the sky, trillions of deadly radioactive particles began to fall. They fell soundlessly, settling like an invisible snow on the devastated earth.

....

There were those whose fate it was to wander this landscape of poisonous desolation. One of them was me.

Robert Swindells
Brother in the Land

Write 2/3 paragraphs using the title ***Nuclear Holocaust***.

H.L. Essay Writing

STAGE 3

Paragraphs

You are not yet ready to write several pages of foolscap on Leaving Certificate essay titles. So where do you begin?

You begin by writing good short passages and gradually building up to a long essay. For the present, let's set the limit at 50 words, and, to make the writing easier still, your 50 words can be a little story, if you wish.

Take one of the following titles and write a paragraph about 50 words long. (Think hard about the possibilities of the titles before you write).

The Postcard	The Home-Coming	Saturday Shopping
Happiness	The Hero	Old Age

Here are some "mini-sagas" from writers whose instructions were to write a story in exactly 50 words. The first one was written by Frederick Forsyth when the Sunday Telegraph magazine held its first mini-saga competition in 1982.

Frederick Forsyth explains how Crime In The City began

"As a writer, one tries to be economical with words. But a whole story in fifty, is almost impossible to achieve. *Crime In The City* took me perhaps an hour to write, and that was spent cutting it down. I tried for one single idea with a twist in the tail. In most stories, the twist alone is more than fifty words. I had learned from someone that gangsters of the Kray type are extremely disapproving of random violence and that, when they ruled the East End, muggers were almost unheard of. My idea was to pit the crime of the mugger against the much more professional crime of the gang hoodlum.

 I get a lot of requests for articles and short stories, but I've never been asked to write anything in fifty words before. I did it because it seemed a challenge. It is an interesting competition for a magazine to run."

Crime In The City

They negotiated in the limousine. Neat, dark business suits. Professional men. The radio news carried another mugging: pensioner savaged in Brixton. "Disgusting," said one; "no law and order any more." The other memorised the photograph of a contract, a welsher. "Tell the client, 24 hours and it's done." Professional men.

H.L. Essay Writing

1. What the Sleeping Beauty would have given her right arm for.

The princess was different. She was a brunette beauty with a genius of a brain. Refusing marriage, she inherited all by primogeniture. The country's economy prospered under her rule. When the handsome prince came by on his white charger, she bought it from him and started her own racehorse business.

2. Out of the Mouths of Babes?

"Come and meet my friend on sports day, mummy."
Sports day came.
"Where's your new friend Paul?"
"He's sitting on the front bench."
There were ten on the front bench.
"He's wearing red shorts."
There were three boys with red shorts.
"His hair's curly."
"Oh, the black one," said mummy.

3. Smile Though Your Heart is Faking

He wasn't all there. Tactfully, they concealed his wellingtons. Weeds choked the allotment. Grateful, he plucked the dahlias from carpets; offered transparent bouquets. Disbelieved, they went unwatered. He wilted. Bedfast, he captured butterflies, exhibiting empty hands. Heads shook. Leaves were taken. Tributes feigned. Gone, he pushes up their plastic roses.

4. Saturday Shopping

Home at last, light the gas fire, fill the kettle. All that planning had paid off. Silly women acting on impulse always get caught. Not her. Life would be different now, have some meaning. The bundle in the holdall stirred. Rock it gently. "Sssh little love, you are mine now..."

5. The Hero

Yellow banners came down from the mountains. Triumphant soldiery poured into the capital city. Everywhere, cheering citizens, waving flags. Their great rebel leader, their hero, appeared on the Rathaus steps. "This day marks a new epoch in the history of our nation," he shouted. So began twenty years of tyranny.

6. Home-coming

"Good to have you back son," the old man said.
"Nice to be back."
"You've had a rough time," The eyes clouded with guilt. "Hope you don't think I let you down."
The younger shook his head.
"You warned me, dad. But it wasn't the nails. It was the kiss."

H.L. Essay Writing

7. The Postcard

Friendless, he despatched a letter to the twelfth century. Illuminated scrolls arrived by return post. Jottings to Tutankhamun secured hieroglyphics on papyrus; Hannibal sent a campaign report. But when he addressed the future, hoping for cassettes crammed with wonders, a postcard drifted back with scorched edges. It glowed all night.

All of the mini-sagas numbered 1-7 above were prizewinners in a newspaper competition. Place them in order of merit, and justify your choice of top prizewinners.

The following mini-sagas were written by 5th year students. Choose which you think are the two best and give reasons for your choices.

The Home-coming

The huge, intergalactic vessel plummeted through the dimensions of space, searching. They had come to the edge of space and time on their lonely vigil. They had passed great civilisations and worlds without interest. Now they approached the rich, fertile planet which their forefathers had been forced to leave aeons ago. Earth!

Tomb

The stone was heaved aside, an eerie gust of wind blew, still smelling of papyrus. All the wealth of Egypt lay inside; but at what cost? Shadows trembled. Natives fled crying "blasphemy!" Archaeologists stayed: twentieth century bodysnatchers.

Crime in the City

He was safe. No one would try anything here. He had finally outmanoeuvred them. In the mall, he would be lost in the crowd.
Outside, two men were speaking. "You know what to do." Minutes later, both walked quickly away.
In their wake, dust plumes rose high as the mall disappeared.

H.L. Essay Writing

Crime in the City

The precision of an arithmetican's perfect crime. Can it be executed? Silent driver, nervous partner.
They approach dim, grey vaults. The stress is unbearable. Hot torches rip through metal caving.
The priceless haul is loaded. Fast getaway.
A voice cuts the silence "Hi, I'm detective Baynes. Meet Sgt. Stephens," says the driver.

A Family Affair

The family had gathered in the library to hear Uncle Ernest's last will and testament. Charles, uncle's favourite nephew, smiled at everyone. Tense faces. It took Mr. Hunter Davies just 3 minutes to dispose of the 3 million estate.
What the Bellevue Home for Distressed Cats would make of it was anyone's guess.

A. Now write some mini-sagas of your own, using the following titles.

- Power
- Magic
- Memories
- Death
- Celebration
- Schooldays
- Loneliness
- City Life
- Gossip

B. Write 50 word paragraphs or stories, using the following first lines as starting points.

a) Night was falling .....
b) Heavy footsteps were approaching ...
c) Dustbin lids rattled along the pavement ......
d) As they crawled through the undergrowth .....
e) The city hummed with life .....
f) Day was breaking .....
g) Lifeless .....
h) Afterwards, he knew it had all been a mistake ...
i) Far away in the distance, she could hear the sound of ...

H.L. Essay Writing

Opening Paragraphs

B. Listen to some great authors' opening lines. Well-read people will be able to match authors and titles!

1. "Marley was dead, to begin with. There is no doubt whatever about that."

2. "It was in the Spring of the year 1894 that all London was interested, and the fashionable world dismayed, by the murder of the honourable Ronald Adair under the most unusual and inexplicable circumstances."

3. "If you really want to hear about it, the first thing you'll probably want to know is where I was born, and what my lousy childhood was like.. but I don't feel like going into it."

4. "In my younger and more vulnerable years my father gave me some advice that I've been turning over in my mind ever since."

5. "The boys when they talked to the girls from Marcia Blaine school stood on the far side of their bicycles holding the handlebars, which established a protective fence of bicycle between the sexes, and the impression that at any moment the boys were likely to be away."

6. "Man is a born liar."

7. "In the year 1872, the house, no. 7 Sackville Row, Burlington Gdns., was occupied by Phileas Fogg Esq."

(a) *Liam O'Flaherty, "A Tourist's Guide to Ireland."*

(b) *Scott Fitzgerald, "The Great Gatsby."*

(c) *J.R. Tolkien, "The Lord of the Rings."*

(d) *Charles Dickens, "A Christmas Carol."*

(e) *J. D. Salinger, "The Catcher in the Rye."*

(f) *William Trevor, "A School Story."*

(g) *Muriel Spark, "The Prime of Miss Jean Brodie."*

H.L. Essay Writing

8. "Every night, after lights out in the dormitory, there was a ceremonial story-telling."

(h) Sir Arthur Conan Doyle, "The Adventure of the Empty House."

9. "The tourist is at the mercy of every kind of ruffian."

(i) Jules Verne, "Around the World in Eighty Days."

10. "This book is largely concerned with Hobbits."

(j) Liam O'Flaherty, "Shame the Devil."

Now take one of the above opening lines and continue it to make a good opening for an essay.

Let's listen to 3 fiction writers' opening paragraphs.

Denis's school was in the heart of the country, miles from anywhere, and this gave the teachers an initial advantage, because before a boy even got to the railway station he had the prefects on his track. Two fellows Denis knew once got as far as Mellin, a town ten miles off, intending to join the British Army, but like fools the first thing they did in Mellin was to go to a hotel, so they were caught in bed in the middle of the night by prefects and brought back. It was reported that they had been flogged on their knees in front of the picture of the Crucifixion in the hall, but no one was ever able to find out the truth about that. Denis thought they must have been inspired by the legend of two fellows who did once actually get on a boat for England and were never heard of afterwards, but that was before his time, and in those days escapes were probably easier. By the time he got there it was said there was a telescope mounted on the tower and that the prefects took turns at watching for fellows trying to get away.

Frank O'Connor

Pity

The accused, Patrick Haughy, went into the witness-box and was duly sworn. Just as he was about to begin his statement, District Justice Murnihan interrupted him:
"What did you say your name was?" said the Justice.
The accused was a very disreputable young tinker with red hair and a pointed chin.
"Patrick Haughy, yer honour," he said.
"Oh!" said the Justice. "What I mean is, how do you spell it?"
"Begob," said the Tinker, shrugging his shoulders, "I never spelt it in me life."
There was laughter in court.
District Superintendent Clarke informed the Justice that the name was spelt H-a-u-g-h-y.
"Oh!" said the Justice. "In that case I should think the correct pronunciat on is Aw-Hee."
"Or would it be Och-ee?" said the Justice. "There were Irish kings of that name."
"Yer honour," said the accused, "I was arrested by the pronunciation of Haw-Hee."
There was further laughter in court. The accused then began his statement.

Liam O'Flaherty

The Stolen Ass

H.L. Essay Writing

My grandmother made dying her life's work. I remember her as a vast malevolent old woman, so obese that she was unable to wander beyond the paved yard outside her front door. Her pink-washed cottage had two rooms and she agonised her way through and around them, clutching at the furniture for support and emitting heart-scalding gasps, as if death was no further off than the dresser or the settle bed where my uncle Sonny slept himself sober. In those days people confused old age with valour; they called her a great old warrior. This had the effect of inspiring her to gasp even more distressingly by way of proving them right and herself indomitable. In case her respiratory noises should come to be as taken for granted as the ticking of the clock (which at least stopped now and then), she provided a contrapuntal accompaniment by kicking the chairs, using the milk jugs as cymbals and percussing the kettle and frying pan.

To be fair, it was her only diversion. The rent-man, peering in over the half-door, would suffer like a damned soul as she counted out three shillings and ninepence in coppers, threepenny bits and sixpences, wheezing a goodbye to each coin, and then began her tortured via dolorosa towards him, determined to pay her debts before dropping dead at his feet, a martyr to landlordism. Even Dr. Enright was intimidated. When he had listened to her heartbeats it was not his stethoscope but her doomed slaughterhouse eyes imploring the worst which caused him to tell her: 'Sure we've all got to go some day, ma'am.' That pleased her. Privately, she saw no reason why she should go at any time, but she liked to nod submissively, essay a practice death-rattle and resignedly endorse the will of the Almighty.

She dressed in shiny black and wore a brooch inscribed 'Mother.' Her girth almost exceeded her stature, and her prodigious appetite amazed me, for her cooking verged on the poisonous.

Hugh Leonard
Home Before Night

Now discuss each of the above 3 openings, using the following guidelines.

1. Is the author arousing interest in the reader?
2. Has he created a mood or atmosphere in a few lines?
3. What do you like/dislike about the style of writing?
4. Would you be interested enough to read on?

H.L. Essay Writing

More Opening Lines

Your opening lines in an essay are crucial. They give your examiner a first impression of your writing ability. So give them power, wit, personality and style!

Depending on the type of essay you are writing, you may want your opening lines to do different things. A good opening line may:

a) Make an important, serious statement which you intend developing in the rest of your essay.

b) Amuse the reader.

c) Arouse the reader's curiosity.

d) Set an atmosphere or mood.

Watch people in a library. They take a book from the shelf, read the first few lines and then either keep the book or replace it, depending on how the opening lines have gripped them. Your examiner has no choice but to read on, even if your opening lines are as dull as can be. But you've made an impression for good or ill with your first words.

Here are some examples of opening lines. Give each one the grade you think it deserves, then write your own opening line and grade it also.

A. outstanding   **C.** good   **E.** poor

B. very good   **D.** fair

Title		**Opening Lines**
1. *Roads*	(a)	There is ten times as much traffic on our roads now as there was a few years go.
	(b)	Why did the chicken cross the road? Was it to satisfy his little spirit of adventure?
	(c)	When I was a child, the small road I lived on seemed to stretch for miles.
		Now write your own first line on *Roads* and grade it.

33

H.L. Essay Writing

2. *Money is the root of all evil*

   (a) Bible-thumping preachers, nuns in quiet cloisters and Salvation Army singers all proclaim the wickedness of money. But, who, I ask you, could live happily without it?..............

   (b) Most proverbs are nonsense posing as wisdom, but this one contains a grain of truth...............

   (c) It is a well-known fact that rich people lead unhappy lives. A kid from a rich home is probably lonely and spoiled................................

   Write your own and grade it.

3. *Sounds by night*

   (a) Ever since the beginning of time, the night has been a time of fear and mystery.........................

   (b) Cats wail in narrow alleyways, dustbin lids rattle and papers rustle along deserted streets. The city sleeps..

   (c) Close your eyes and listen to the night. Open your ears to the soft lapping of water, the whisper of dark trees, the crack of stone and the vast brooding silence of the moonlight................

   Write your own and grade it.

4. *The horrors of the modern city*

   (a) The good Samaritan is an extinct species..........

   (b) There is so much pollution now that the city centre is a horrible place to live in.....................

   (c) "Get off the road, thickhead!" roared the irate taxi driver as the learner driver struggled with the gear box...

   Write your own and grade it.

H.L. Essay Writing

5. *School*
   (a) School is a place where they make you go and tell you what to do and where they make your life miserable if you don't do it right..............
   (b) School can be happy or unhappy, depending on the type of person you are........................
   (c) The school building was tall and ugly. Clare didn't like the way it made her feel inside.......

   Write your own and grade it.

6. *Modern architecture*
   (a) Modern architecture seems to be whatever self-appointed prophets believe will be all the rage in twenty years time...........................
   (b) Modern architecture is a monstrous shrine, built in honour of the three gods; glass, steel and cement..

   Write your own and grade it.

7. *Christmas*
   (a) Christmas, season of long queues and short tempers, fills me with annual dread..............
   (b) "Tis the season to be jolly..." If you're a publican, toyshop owner or turkey farmer; otherwise, Christmas is about as much fun as a football riot...

   Write your own and grade it.

8. What comments would you make on the following opening sentences for an essay entitled *International sport*?
   (a) Since the dark ages, man has participated in sporting events in one form or another...
   (b) When you look at this title and take it in, your mind just seems to wander and it is so difficult to know where to start..
   (c) There are many things which could be described as international sport, but the one which instantly comes to mind is World Cup Soccer................................

H.L. Essay Writing

(d) There are two sides to sport, as with everything else; the good side and the bad side..

(e) International sport is one of the most widely used forms of communication between various realms in today's nationalist world..

(f) Today, the world of international sport has become a world of cold professionals, intent on winning at any cost..

Take one of the eight titles:

1. Roads
2. Money is the root of all evil
3. Sounds by night
4. The horrors of the modern city
5. School
6. Modern architecture
7. Christmas
8. International Sport

and write an introductory paragraph on the title you've chosen.

Ending Your Essay

Examiners complain that many candidates' essays either end abruptly or merely peter out. The candidate obviously tires of the whole subject and wants to finish. It is a pity to spoil a good essay with a weak ending in this way. As with the beginning of your essay, the ending should be strong and impressive and give your reader a sense of completeness.

So What Can You Do?

- You can go back to your opening statement and echo it with slight changes. This can be very effective and gives your essay a sense of unity. It gives the impression of having brought your essay full circle.
  For example an essay entitled "Money is the root of all evil" that began with the sentence,
  "Bible-thumping preachers, nuns in quiet cloisters and Salvation Army singers all proclaim the wickedness of money. But who, I ask you, could live happily without it?"

  might end with the lines,

  "Even as I write this essay, those preachers, nuns and singers are all living happily without money ... but ask yourself honestly. Could you?"

- You can end with an appropriate quotation, e.g.
  In the words of Sean O'Casey "Money doesn't buy happiness, but a little helps to calm the nerves."

- You can end with a strong statement which tries to sum up the points you've been making:
  "It would seem to me that, far from being the root of all evil, money can be a force for great good in a harsh world."

- You must always come to a genuine conclusion. Never give the impression that you have merely come to a halt.

H.L. Essay Writing

If you read fiction, you will have noticed that good writers manage to give a powerful atmosphere in concluding lines. Here are Daphne du Maurier's closing paragraphs of her famous story "The Birds." (This story became an Alfred Hitchcock classic film).

The cottage was filled with stores, with fuels, with all they needed for the next few days. When he had finished dinner he would put the stuff away, stack it neatly, get everything shipshape, handy-like. His wife could help him, and the children too. They'd tire themselves out, between now and a quarter to nine, when the tide would ebb; then he'd tuck them down on their mattresses, see that they slept good and sound until three in the morning.

He had a new scheme for the windows, which was to fix barbed wire in front of the boards. He had brought a great roll of it from the farm. The nuisance was, he'd have to work at this in the dark, when the lull came between nine and three. Pity he had not thought of it before. Still, as long as the wife slept, and the kids, that was the main thing.

The smaller birds were at the windows now. He recognized the light tap-tapping of their beaks and the soft brush of their wings. The hawks ignored the windows. They concentrated their attack upon the door. Nat listened to the tearing sound of splintering wood, and wondered how many million years of memory were stored in those little brains, behind the stabbing beaks, the piercing eyes, now giving them this instinct to destroy mankind with all the deft precision of machines.

"I'll smoke that last fag," he said to his wife. "Stupid of me, it was the thing I forgot to bring back from the farm."
He searched for it, switched on the silent wireless. He threw the empty packet on the fire, and watched it burn.

1. *The family in the story has tried to fortify their cottage against the birds' attack. The author manages to show you very subtly, that the father, Nat, thinks the situation is hopeless. How is this hopeless mood created?*

2. *Which, in your opinion, is the most **dramatic** paragraph here? What makes it so?*

3. *Think carefully about the closing sentence. This ending is inconclusive. Some readers might be dissatisfied with it. Are you?*

H.L. Essay Writing

This is James Joyce's ending for his short story, "The Dead." It is Christmas time, after midnight, and Joyce is catching that quiet atmosphere as snow falls, in the still of the night.

A few light taps upon the pane made him turn to the window. It had begun to snow again. He watched sleepily the flakes, silver and dark, falling obliquely against the lamplight. The time had come for him to set out on his journey westward. Yes, the newspapers were right: snow was general all over Ireland. It was falling on every part of the dark central plain, and the treeless hills, falling softly upon the Bog of Allen and, farther westward, softly falling into the dark mutinous Shannon waves. It was falling, too, upon every part of the lonely churchyard on the hill where Michael Furey lay buried. It lay thickly drifted on the crooked crosses and headstones, on the spears of the little gate, on the barren thorns. His soul swooned slowly as he heard the snow falling faintly through the universe and faintly falling, like the descent of their last end, upon all the living and the dead.

James Joyce

1. *This paragraph is often described as poetic. What makes it so in your opinion?*
   (Consider imagery, use of repetition, "s" sounds to give that gentle effect of softly falling snow.........................
2. *Write a paragraph entitled "Snow."*

Descriptive Paragraphs

You've been writing and reading **Narrative** passages in the last few lessons. It is good to develop some skill in **Descriptive** writing also, in order to create mood or atmosphere in your writing.

To the farthest skyline it was Sunday. The valley walls were neat .. postcard pretty. The blue sky, the sparkling, smokeless Sunday air, had disinfected them. Picnickers were already up there, sprinkled like confetti along the steep lanes and paths.

Life, over the whole countryside was suspended for the day.

Ted Hughes

1. *Underline what you think are the two most striking words or phrases in this passage.*
2. *Write a paragraph entitled "Sunday."*

H.L. Essay Writing

This was my second spring in the Dales but it was like the one before — and all the springs after. The kind of spring, that is, that a country vet knows; the din of the lambing pens, the bass rumble of the ewes and the high, insistent bawling of the lambs. This for me, has always heralded the end of winter and the beginning of something new. This and the piercing Yorkshire wind and the hard, bright sunshine flooding the bare hillsides.

There had been a change during the last week; the harsh winds had dropped, everything had softened and greened and the warming land gave off its scents. On the lower slopes of the fell, in the shade of the woods, a pale mist of bluebells drifted among the dead bronze of the bracken and their fragrance came up to me on the breeze.

James Herriot

It was a sweet, hot day in May, the grass already long and deep, with golden cowslips rising everywhere among the tombstones, and bluebells hanging like dark smoke under the creamy waterfalls of hawthorn bloom.

Mark Twain

The summer world was bright and fresh and brimming with life. There was a song in every heart, cheer in every face and a spring in every step. The trees and flowers were in bloom and the fragrance of blossoms filled the air. The countryside was dreamy, sun-drenched and inviting.

Mark Twain

H.L. Essay Writing

September and October are said to be the worst months of the year in Leningrad. A raw damp wind blows in from the Gulf of Finland, fog and rain follow one another in a depressing succession of days, and everywhere mud and slush lie underfoot. It is often dark in the early afternoon and the cold night continues until nine or ten in the morning.

But then in November something perfectly wonderful happens: the heavy snow begins. It falls so thickly and so persistently that it blocks the view a few yards ahead, and sometimes in the course of a single night the whole city is transformed. The mud vanishes and the gold spires and coloured cupolas now stand out against a background of dazzling whiteness. There is a kind of joy in the air. The temperature may stand well below zero, but in this dry sparkling atmosphere people get rid of their coughs and colds at last and can afford to smile.

Alan Moorehead

We stepped out into the Winter world. It was a world of glass, sparkling and motionless. Everything was rigid, locked up and sealed, and when we breathed the air it smelt like needles and stabbed our nostrils. The old trees sparkled like tinsel and the world was quiet.

Laurie Lee

Winter is always the worst time in the city. In Autumn, the trees along suburban roads are venerable but elegant; in Winter, they are gnarled and ragged ancients with rheumatic knuckles and bones. The east wind beats in from the sea and drives under the arches of the river.

James Plunkett

1. Each of the 7 descriptive paragraphs above is trying to capture the mood of a particular time of the year. Which, in your opinion, is most successful? Give reasons for your choice.
2. Write paragraphs using the titles:
Spring
Summer
Autumn
Winter

H.L. Essay Writing

Gathering Words and Phrases

Take as our title,

A dingy street in a run-down city area.

Try to imagine the scene for yourself and picture the street. You can then systematically gather material under useful headings:

Buildings

crooked doorways
barbed wire on flat roofs
derelict warehouses with *For Sale* signs

cracked windows
broken shutters
old scrapyard
small newsagents

playground fenced off with corrugated iron
derelict houses... rotting timber
betting shop... skeletons of houses
dingy social welfare office

peeling paint on windows

tumbledown shops
cracked pavements

patch of wasteland littered with rubble
boards nailed over windows
iron girders holding up walls

chip shop

hills of rubble

Small details

dead bluebottles in shop windows
bins and plastic sacks
grey washing hanging from windows
broken drainpipes
weeds growing from cracks in walls
dandelions jutting from chimney pots
burnt out cars
trampled cardboard boxes
old window boxes with dead flowers

cigarette butts and tin cans in gutters
smashed street lamps

graffiti on walls
broken railings

stagnant pools of water
torn posters on walls

shopping trolley with no wheels in alleyway

People: (Young & Old)

Hawkers selling clothes/sweets/fruit
old men sitting on battered armchairs in doorways
squealing children kicking a burst football
boys on home-made stilts
old tramp rummaging in bin
women with torn shopping bags
people queuing at social welfare office
old faces at windows
men slipping in the dark
doorway of betting shop/pub
teenagers leaning against chip shop windows
women chatting and pointing at new houses
across the playground
postman on pushbike
mothers pushing prams with shopping hanging from sides

Animals

dogs tearing at plastic sacks
skinny stray cats hissing and fighting
birds' nests among disused chimney tops
ratholes in dilapidated walls
cats prowling, dogs howling

1. Now, using some of the words and phrases above, write 2 paragraphs, beginning with the words,

   As I turned off the main street, I found myself in a dingy, dilapidated world ....

2. Using the headings above, (Buildings .... small details ... people ... animals), gather words and phrases for 2 paragraphs describing,

   "An elegant street in an expensive area of the city."
   Then, write 2 paragraphs beginning,
   "As I turned the corner, I found myself in a very elegant world ...."

H.L. Essay Writing

Writers Creating Atmosphere

THE GRAPES OF WRATH
JOHN STEINBECK

> Then it was June, and the sun shone more fiercely. The dirt crust broke and the dust formed. Every moving thing lifted a thin layer as high as his waist, and a wagon lifted the dust as high as the fence tops.
>
> The air and the sky darkened and through them the sun shone redly, and there was a raw sting in the air. Little by little the sky was darkened by the mixing dust, and the wind felt over the earth, loosened the dust, and carried it away. The wind grew stronger. The rain crust broke and the dust lifted up out of the fields and drove grey plumes into the air like sluggish smoke.
>
> Men and women huddled in their houses, and they tied handkerchiefs over their noses when they went out, and wore goggles to protect their eyes.
>
> When the night came again it was black night, for the stars could not pierce the dust and get down, and the window lights could not even spread beyond their own yards. Houses were shut tight, and cloth wedged around doors and windows, but the dust came in so thinly that it could not be seen in the air, and it settled like pollen on the chairs and tables, on the dishes.
>
> In the morning the dust hung like fog and the sun was as red as ripe new blood. All day the dust sifted down from the sky, and the next day it sifted down. An even blanket covered the earth. It settled on the corn, piled up on the tops of the fence posts, piled up on the wires; it settled on roofs, blanketed the weeds and trees.
>
> The people came out of their houses and smelled the hot stinging air and covered their noses from it. And the children came out of the houses, but they did not run or shout as they would have done after a rain. Men stood by their fences and looked at the ruined corn, dying fast now, only a little green showing through the film of dust.
>
> *John Steinbeck*

1. Give this passage a title.
2. Which 3 phrases in the passage impress you most?
3. What 2 adjectives would you use to describe the mood or atmosphere here?
4. Write a passage using "Rain" as the dominant word.

H.L. Essay Writing

THE RETURN OF THE KING
J. R. R. TOLKIEN

> There was a long silence, and from wall and gate no cry or sound was heard in answer. As the Captains were about to turn away, the silence was broken suddenly. There came a long rolling of great drums like thunder in the mountains. And thereupon the middle door of the Black Gate was thrown open with a great clang, and out of it there came an embassy from the Dark Tower.
>
> At its head there rode a tall and evil shape, mounted upon a black horse, if horse it was; for it was huge and hideous, and its face was a frightful mask, more like a skull than a living head, and in the sockets of its eyes and in its nostrils there burned a flame. The rider was robed all in black, and black was his lofty helm; yet this was no Ringswraith but a living man.
>
> But it is told that he was a renegade, who came of the race of those that were named the Black Numenoreans; for they established their dwellings in Middle-earth during the years of Sauron's domination, and they worshipped him, being enamoured of evil knowledge.
>
> *J. R. R. Tolkien*

1. Give this passage a title.
2. Which 3 phrases in the passage impress you most?
3. What two adjectives would you use to describe the atmosphere here?
4. Write a passage using either "dark" or "black" as the dominant word.

H.L. Essay Writing

Discursive Paragraphs

You've now tried writing **Narrative** and **Descriptive** paragraphs. Let's turn to a different type of writing skill — giving your opinions. Novel reading helps to develop good narrative and descriptive writing skills and also feeds your imagination so you see more possibilities in essay titles. But how do you go about improving your ability to discuss a topic currently in the news or to argue a point of view?

You should develop the habit of reading quality newspapers and magazines which keep you informed and open your mind to discussion. Taking part in school debates is also an excellent way of developing your ability to argue and express your opinions.

Look at what the various critics write in the newspapers. It is their job to give opinions in print. They write reviews of music, theatre, television and radio, videos, books, restaurants and all sorts of public entertainments, from street festivals to concerts. Writing your own reviews will help you to develop a critical style.

Look at the following examples:

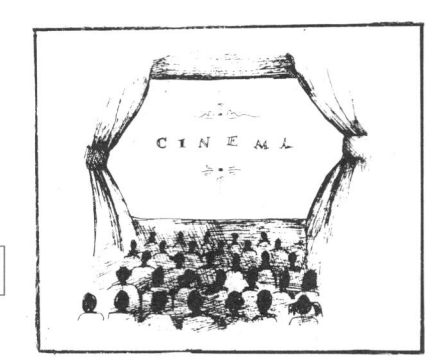

Cinema

"Murder by Proxy"

This new thriller from the Italian director, Paul Bertolucci is lifted above the ordinary by the outstanding performances of Al Visconti and Meryl Long. It offers a new twist to the old "strangler-in-the-night" theme and keeps you on the edge of your seat till the closing minutes. The photography is excellent and Bertolluci manages to capture perfectly the atmosphere of New York in the 1940s. It won't be a blockbuster but it is a well-crafted piece of cinema entertainment at its best.

Write a review (100 words approx) of a film you saw recently.

H.L. Essay Writing

Book Reviews

The Homecoming, by Jean Kelly

13 year old Michael runs away from a children's home in Birmingham. He believes he was born in Galway and goes in search of his family. The novel traces his journey across the Irish Sea, through Dublin and the midlands as Michael learns how to survive and fend for himself.

There is a very unusual twist-in-the-tail ending as Michael finds Galway and home. Younger readers will love it.

Sweet Success by Jay Ellman is very difficult to sum up in a few sentences. Jay Ellmann is an American writer now living in Dublin and his novel is set in Ireland in the 1970s. His hero is a "rags to riches" businessman whose life becomes complicated when he is approached by a member of an illegal organisation to help in an arms deal. The story that follows is well told and gripping to the end. The scenes of Irish life are realistic and readers will enjoy identifying familiar faces and places. I found the romantic element very unconvincing and superfluous. Perhaps the publisher demanded it, but it spoils an otherwise realistic work.

Armageddon by Sean Stephens

The earth smoulders under scorching heat. Rain and heavy floods destroy arable land. "Multi-megaton hurricanes" and "gigawatt thunderstorms" besiege our polluted, rotten planet.

The world of politics is just as chaotic as the dying planet. A nuclear flashpoint seems imminent. Total eclipse of the sun will occur on "bombfire night" November 5th. The main character who tells the story is dying of radiation sickness in this terrible world.

This novel is not for the faint-hearted. It is dark, savage and gruesome and shows urban squalor at its worst.

Write a book review (100 words approx.) Use the most recent book you read or an old favourite you read in the past.

H.L. Essay Writing

Radio and Television

Gerry Kenny's new morning show is a magazine type mixture of music, phone-ins, interviews and news reviews. On Monday last, he spoke to a woman who had lost 5 stone in one year and has now published a book called "The Slimmer You." Can the market really take another diet book? Five minutes with these "miracle diet" people is four minutes too long and Gerry should stop asking inane questions like, "Is life different when you are fat?"

Margaret Murray, a new voice on R.T.E., brought some interesting angles on the big news stories of the week. No great controversies arose from the phone-ins but the man from Bray who complained about his neighbour's habit of throwing cinders over the garden wall made his point very clearly. Let's hope that his slovenly, inconsiderate neighbour was listening!

Olivia Byrne's documentary on a day in the life of a homeless man in the streets of Cork was a wonderful piece of television. No sensationalism here, just an honest look at a typical day in the life of someone outside of respectable society. The questions posed were simple and direct, the man was articulate and unemotional in presenting his dilemma. How does a person become "employable" from so desperate a situation? This was television at its best.

Write a review (100 words approx.) of a television or radio programme that you saw or heard in the past week.

H.L. Essay Writing

Write your reaction to the following newspaper articles (200 words approx. in each case).

Jailed soccer thugs freed

Ten Swansea soccer fans found guilty of vandalising thousands of pounds worth of property prepared to leave Greece yesterday after they bought off their prison sentences, authorities said.

The Swansea City soccer club supporters each paid £800 over the last two days to buy off 16-month jail terms for damaging property during a drunken rampage in an Athens suburb last Friday.

At least six of the fans were waiting to return to Britain yesterday, a British Embassy spokesman said.

Vicky Economou, a lawyer representing the Welshmen, said four of them were on their way to the capital after they were released earlier yesterday from a prison at Khalkis, 55 miles north of Athens.

The Swansea City fans were arrested after a drunken rampage through the Athens coastal resort of Glyfada which led to about £8,000 worth of damage to three tavernas.

Panathinaikos of Athens beat Swansea 3-2 last Wednesday in a European Cupwinners' Cup match.

The Swansea fans claimed in court last Saturday they were attacked by Greeks as they "celebrated after the match."

H.L. Essay Writing

The Plastic Peril in the Sea

Like a good many other beachcombers, I suppose, I have been living with plastic trash so long that I have almost ceased to see it — rather as citydwellers learn to screen out the litter of their streets. Much of it, by an irony that should touch us more sharply, consists of containers from the household cleansing industry: we clean up our immediate environment only to pollute the seas and beaches. But new categories of plastic debris are being added all the time.

Plastic is killing the turtles, — especially the everyday, all purpose plastic bag. As it floats in the ocean, just beneath the surface, the bag swells with water, pulsating as it drifts. It is, for all the world a jellyfish, which is what turtles eat. Of 15 leatherback turtles found washed ashore dead in one fortnight on Long Island, 11 had plastic bags blocking their stomach openings.

Monofilament fishing net is almost invisible in water and lasts for years. Nets discarded at sea or lost in storms become "ghostnets," still catching fish and entangling their predators. In one such net of 1,500 metres, recovered after a month, there were 99 seabirds, over 200 salmon or their skeletons, and a couple of sharks. In the North Pacific, 30,000 northern fur seals die each year, trapped in the 600-odd miles of monofilament gill net lost or discarded by the Japanese fishing fleet.

Plastic six-pack rings are throttling birds and maiming fish; plastic balloons, released en masse for charity, are ultimately swallowed as "jellyfish;" polystyrene foam cups disintegrate into granules which turn up in impacted stomachs and crops of seabirds. This summer, a research yacht sailed from New York to Leningrad, dragging a small net behind it for 30 minutes everyday. It dredged up plastic debris from every haul except one, with an average of ten bits per tow.

Do you want the figures on the plastic garbage dumped at sea from trawlers, pleasure craft, cruise liners, merchantmen, oil tankers, aircraft-carriers? The US Navy has agreed to stop dumping kitchen-galley wrappers, bags and straps by 1992, thus reducing the ocean's burden by a modest 5.4 tons per day. There is, of course, an international convention on dumping garbage at sea, something called MARPOL for short — which, I gather we haven't signed. There is a Marine Pollution Bill somewhere in the pipeline, but in the meantime how many Irish harbours even provide a skip to take rubbish from visiting ships?

Seaborne plastic is no longer just a gripe of middle-class aesthetics; it is killing wildlife in pathetic and horrible ways. And far from declining, as we thought it might in the days when oil seemed "finite", the use of plastic in everyday, disposable products is expanding dramatically (Coca-Cola USA, for example, have been test-marketing plastic "cans;" Campbells is selling soups in microwave-ready plastic bowls).

Those pellets down in the neighbour's field — a tiny handful among billions — have nothing, of course, to do with anyone round here. Except that, like everyone else, we go on expecting the environment to absorb the products made from them, ad infinitum. In the suffering of seals and birds and turtles and whales, we begin to see some of the cost.

Is this writer making his points strongly? Which points impress you particularly? Do you agree with him?

H.L. Essay Writing

Gangs with knives on rampage on streets of Dublin

Gangs of roving youths, brandishing knives and binoculars have been responsible for a sudden increase in stabbings in Dublin city centre, according to an investigation by the Sunday Tribune.

A Garda spokesman denied that there was any increase in frightening knife attacks in the area, but unofficial sources in the force confirm an increasing incidence of such assaults.

The assailants, according to one garda, travel in packs and are able to "pick the most vulnerable to rob and mug." He explained that because there are fewer "on-the-beat" officers there is "little that can be done to prevent such attacks."

Nurses in the emergency ward of one Dublin hospital also confirmed the regular frequency of knife injuries. Every weekend, victims are treated, varying in degrees from the near-fatal wounds to the minor nicks. "The last month, in particular, has been laden with such injuries," she said.

Another garda source indicated that most of these attacks were drug-related, with the proceeds going to feed extensive heroin or cocaine habits.

Write newspaper articles for the following headlines:
1. More Football Violence
2. Waters Polluted
3. Street Violence

H.L. Essay Writing

Letters to the Editor

Many of the essays set on Leaving Certificate papers are about topical issues of interest. Reading letters to the Editor in the daily papers will keep you informed about public opinion.

Dear Editor,
Once again, we must pay an increase in the T.V. licence fee. Since the quality of home-produced programmes continues to deteriorate and we see more and more serialised drivel from the U.S. must the government add insult to injury by asking us to pay more for less?

Is there any good television being produced for the decent, intelligent adult who does not want to be saturated by violence, sentiment, hysterical game-shows and so-called "comedy" shows?

As for the quality of T.V. advertisements — they seem to be aimed at the under 5's.

*Ellen Stephens,
Dublin 12.*

Dear Editor,
Are your readers aware that in recent years, six fishing vessels have been lost in the Irish Sea in unexplained circumstances? Over 20 lives have been lost in these mysterious incidents. The number of documented encounters with submarines totals nine.

The government must take stronger action in its dealings with the British and U.S. navies in these cases. Our fishermen already run great risks and deserve government protection from the hazards of submarines in our waters.

*Selina Gartland,
Lucan.*

Dear Editor,
On a recent trip to Dublin I visited the latest exhibition of modern "art" in the Municipal Gallery. Must the taxpayer support such drivel? We are overtaxed as it is.

*Danny Murray
Rathkeale.*

Write a letter to the editor on a subject about which you feel strongly.

News Items

1. What was the lead story on last night's main evening news?

2. Can you remember 3 news stories that have hit the headlines in the last fortnight?
   a) Briefly, write a headline for each of them.
   b) Write a paragraph on one of the news stories you have just mentioned.

3. Can you name some heads of state at present? Who is head of state (president/prime minister) of each of the following countries:
   a) The United States?
   b) The U.S.S.R?
   c) West Germany?
   d) France?
   e) Britain?
   f) Australia?
   Write a newspaper article (real or imaginary) about one of these leaders.

4. Write an article for a local newspaper, promoting a local club or association to which you belong.

5. Are you a regular reader of a particular newspaper or magazine? Write about this publication, giving your reasons for reading it.

Will You Write For a Living?

Many people earn their living by writing. Perhaps this is the road for you if you write well. Look at these sports articles from the newspapers. Could you write as well as these journalists?

Notice that each article is carefully paragraphed.

The Sports Page

Distribution of Tickets

The person who comes up with an efficient and equitable way to distribute tickets for major sports events will earn the gratitude of all who are genuinely interested in sport. They will certainly earn the gratitude of beleaguered sports journalists who are finding it difficult to distribute the huge bundle of tickets they get for these events.

Without any question, the genuine sports follower is treated badly in these matters. The stories of devoted followers standing disconsolately at their doors watching their ticket-laden neighbours set out for Croke Park are legion. When it comes to getting tickets, those same neighbours, who might not have seen a hurley swung or a ball stick in the course of the year, happen to know somebody who knows somebody and hey presto — two for the Hogan Stand!

So what can be done? It certainly is galling to see so many tickets in the hands of touts before big matches at Croke Park or Landsdowne Road. The success of the Irish soccer team in recent times makes the task of getting tickets very difficult indeed, yet dozens, hundreds, of tickets will be on sale at exorbitant prices right up until the start.

One method of curbing this activity which has been suggested here before would be to pass a law making it illegal to sell tickets above their face value. If laws can be introduced in regard to the price of bread or other commodities surely it would not put too much of a strain on our legal draughtsmen to draw up a bill prohibiting the sale of match tickets, concert tickets, ballet tickets, etc. above the price printed on the ticket itself. This would involve some detective work by plain-clothes gardai on the day of a match but once a few were caught and tickets confiscated, the scourge would soon go away, and with no profits available the touts would disappear.

A ban on the touting, with the force of law behind it, would be a start. That in turn would make it possible to put tickets on sale publicly when a first-come-first-served market would develop and those who were greedy might get caught. It is very doubtful, however, if a fool-proof system to guarantee the genuine follower can be devised. Fair play on the field may be possible but for the present at least, as far as tickets are concerned, there's no justice.

H.L. Essay Writing

CYCLING

Kelly warns today is key day for Earley Cycling

Martin Earley faces the most decisive stage on the Kellogg's Professional Tour of Britain today if he is to retain his overall lead. The 27-year-old Dubliner, now based in Stoke, kept a tight grip on the yellow jersey, despite a second win in three days by West German Remig Stumpf in the 105 miles third stage from Chester to Birmingham yesterday.

Earley, who again relied heavily on his PDM team-mate, Sean Kelly, to control most of the breaks, came home in 28th place in a pack of 66 riders, including Stumpf, who were all given the same time of four hours 10 minutes 32 seconds.

It kept Earley eight seconds ahead of Stumpf, with British professional Malcolm Elliot still in third place, 11 seconds behind.

But with the 62-mile stage criterium around Westminster in London tomorrow including a time bonus of up to 20 seconds for the winner, Kelly warned that his team-mate could be in a difficult position.

"If the race stays as it is at the moment, it's going to be a delicate situation for us and for Martin," said the current World Cup leader. "I don't know why they have decided to award bonuses for the criterium in London. They should give them for the hard days as well."

With the longest stage, a 130-mile ride from Birmingham to Cardiff, including a tough category one climb up the Tumble in Wales today, Kelly added: "We will have to see what the tactics are for that."

Kelly also complained of the poor timing checks on yesterday's stage after Spaniard Mariano Sanchez had got away after 51 miles. "We were told he had a two-minute lead at 20 miles to go when, in fact, he had only 30 to 40 seconds. It meant we had to ride hard to try and catch him when we didn't really need to and I think that was bad."

Aouita is grand prix winner

Quadruple world record holder Said Aouita failed in an attempt to break his 5,000 metres record in the Grand Prix finals in Monte Carlo last night. But his time of 13 minutes 6.36 seconds was enough to give him a comfortable victory and make him the overall winner in the grand prix points table for the year.

Romanian Paula Ivan, who won the mile event last night, retained her overall women's title.

Britain's Colin Jackson ended his losing streak against American world champion Roger Kingdom and boosted his World Cup hopes when he dead-heated in the 110 metres hurdles.

The 22-year-old Jackson had lost his last three outings against the American, but this time Kingdom had to settle for third place as Jackson and American Tonie Campbell both clocked 13.22 seconds.

From the moment the gun fired, Welshman Jackson streaked ahead of Kingdom who had a miserable start. It looked a clearcut victory for Jackson until he clattered the eighth and final hurdles to allow Campbell to draw level, but the fact that he had beaten his archrival was satisfaction enough.

Scotland's Olympic bronze medallist Yvonne Murray had her best win of the season in the 3,000 metres, thanks to a devastating kick 200 metres from the end that left the rest of the world-class field trailing in her wake. Her success last night was worth $10,000.

Steve Backley made it a hat-trick for Britain when he won his seventh javelin grand prix event of the season to prove he is the best in the world. The 20-year-old collected $20,000 for his effort. Backley thus finished third in the overall Grand Prix standings.

Write an article of 3-4 paragraphs for the Sports Page.

H.L. Essay Writing

More Short Pieces of Writing Practice

Gales and Rain

Gales gusting up to 60 miles per hour can be expected today, especially in the west and north-west, according to the Meteorological Service. The average strength of the winds however should be about 35 mph. There will also be spells of rain, turning showery as the day goes on, marking an unpromising start to the October bank holiday weekend.

At sea, the winds are expected to remain at storm force today, particularly on western and northern coasts. The winds are expected to ease off quite significantly by tonight, however, and tomorrow should begin dry. Rain will begin spreading over the country from late morning onwards, reaching all parts by late afternoon and evening. Monday will be brighter, with some sunshine but also showers. Temperatures are expected to be quite low today, but will rise over the rest of the weekend.

Read the newspaper weather forecast and then write your own forecast entitled,

"Sunshine and high temperatures promised for weekend."

EGYPT

16 DAY TOUR OF EGYPT

DEPARTING FROM DUBLIN 15th JANUARY

This Special Holiday Club tour of Egypt explores all the delights this ancient country has to offer. From Cairo you will visit Egypt's pyramids, the massive Sphinx and savour the character of the Bazaar. Then cruise the Nile visiting all the historic sites on your way to the resort of Hurghada where you can enjoy the Aqua Activity Centre at your Sheraton Hotel. Finally, fly back to Cairo and enjoy all it has to offer for a few days.

THAILAND

THAILAND — 14 DAY HOLIDAY

This holiday makes the most of what Thailand has to offer. Enjoy the eastern shopping paradise of Bangkok, famous for its hand woven silks, Thai gold jewellery, ceramics, wood carvings and a multitude of other exquisite hand crafts. You will be given a tour of The Grand Palace and a full day visit of the Floating Markets. To allow you to relax after your four days in Bangkok you'll be escorted to Pattaya Beach just two hours away. This International Playground with its palm fringed beaches and clear blue water is a haven for addicts of sun, sea and sand. You'll spend the remainder of your holidays in Pattaya enjoying the beach, watersports and the easy life-style of Thailand.

CARIBBEAN CRUISE

— 10 DAY HOLIDAY

DEPARTING FROM DUBLIN 2nd DECEMBER

This exclusive holiday on the most luxurious cruise liner in the Caribbean "The Song of America" is the epitome of luxury. As you cruise around the Caribbean you will be wined, dined and entertained in a style you can only dream about. The cruise will take you to Mexico, Grand Cayman, Jamaica and Haiti. You can extend your stay and enjoy the fun of the many Theme Parks and attractions in Florida.

H.L. Essay Writing

Choose a luxurious or exotic holiday destination and write an advertisement for it.

Write an advertisement, directed at the American market, entitled, "Ireland for your next holiday."

Write a news report on an environmental issue. (You could be a reporter speaking from an area where there has been a chemical explosion / serious river pollution / destruction of a forest / oil spillage, etc.)

Write a diary entry for one day in the life of a prisoner.

Write a review of an album / song / piece of music you like.

Write an eye-witness account of the moments leading up to a major accident and the immediate aftermath.

Write a description of a street in a no-go area of a modern city.

Write a description of a landscape after a nuclear explosion.

Write a paragraph from a horror or sci-fi novel in which the author introduces some alien creature(s).

Answers to Opening Lines Quiz on Page 30

1. (d)
2. (h)
3. (e)
4. (b)
5. (g)
6. (j)
7. (i)
8. (f)
9. (a)
10. (c)

STAGE 4
Planning a Full Essay

You must stretch your imagination if you want to interest another person in what you have written. An examiner knows when a candidate is merely filling the page with words. S/he also knows when a candidate has really thought about and developed a subject. It is this development of a subject that is so important.

Narrative writing often seems easier than descriptive or discursive work. In a narrative essay, events may follow each other in a natural time sequence, so you have a ready-made structure for the essay. Of course, you can play around with time and use "flashback" sequences if you wish, but overall, you have a plot to follow and this carries you through from beginning to end. Narrative is interesting if you can successfully create real characters and dramatise events. You may also have a talent for creating atmosphere or suspense. But beware of getting stuck in a rut where you try to turn every title into a story so as to avoid dealing with ideas.

Step 1 is the "Gathering of Ideas"

One way of doing this is to concentrate on a 5 minute "brainstorm" where you take a title and concentrate on it for 5 minutes. Try to think fast and do not raise your pen from the page. Keep Writing!

Let's take two titles, ***Trees***, and ***Hazards of Travel.***

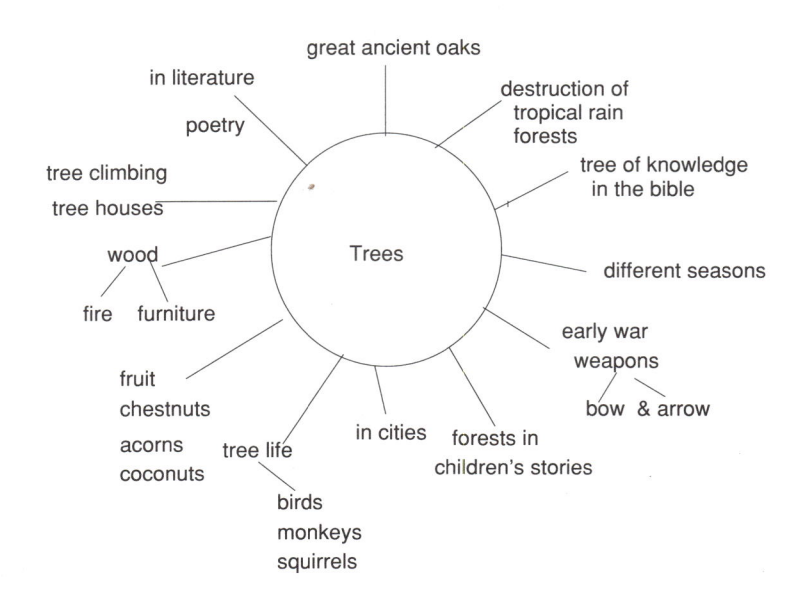

Trees — brainstorm map:
- great ancient oaks
- in literature
- poetry
- destruction of tropical rain forests
- tree of knowledge in the bible
- tree climbing
- tree houses
- different seasons
- wood
- fire
- furniture
- early war weapons
- bow & arrow
- fruit
- chestnuts
- acorns
- coconuts
- tree life
- in cities
- forests in children's stories
- birds
- monkeys
- squirrels

H.L. Essay Writing

```
                        space travel    different modes    planes
            disease                      of travel         ships
                                                           cars
                                              accidents    trains    storms
   political                                                         engine failures
   upheavals                                                         derailments
                          Hazards of
                           Travel                    hijacks
   minor discomforts
   strikes                                                      carriages
   delays                                                       stagecoach
   seasickness                           Past/Present           steam train
                                                                sailing ship
                                                                jet
        Disasters
        Titanic
        Lusitania              Famous Journeys
        Hindenburg
                  Mutiny on Bounty
                       Arctic      Columbus  Marco Polo
                       Expedition
```

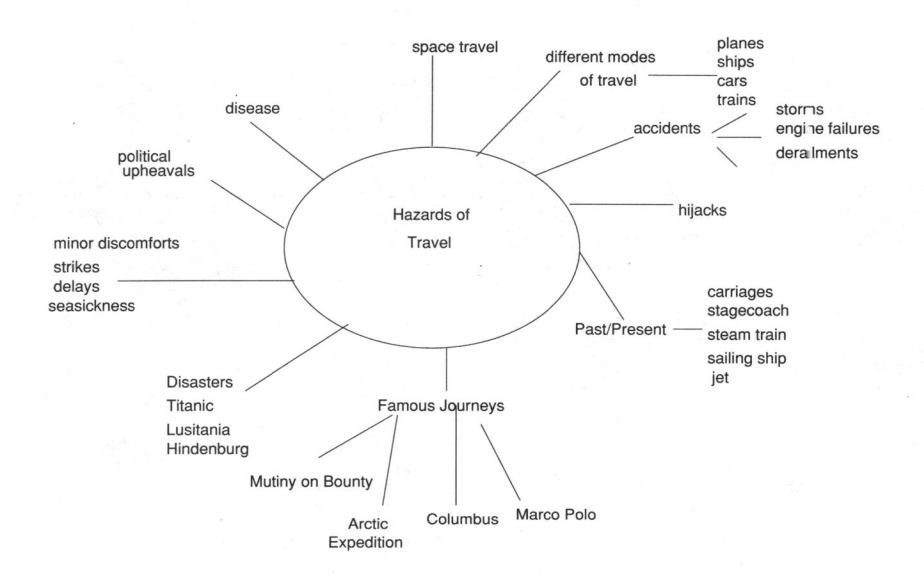

Give yourself 5 minutes for each of the titles below and make diagrams like the ones above.

Streets   *Books*

Music   *Dreams*

Violence   *Science*

Step 2 is Planning and Developing Paragraphs

A paragraph is built around one central idea. You state your theme or idea in the opening or "leader" sentence and you then argue and develop it in the sentences that follow. Then you put a full stop and begin a new paragraph. This may seem elementary, but you would be surprised at how many higher course candidates do not follow this simple rule.

Expand the theme in the following "leader sentences" into a full paragraph:

(a) Public transport is one of the nightmares of modern city life..

(b) The guillotine was a neat little device...

(c) (Name a city you know well) is an exceptionally (use an adjective to describe the city you have named) city ...e.g. Paris is an exceptionally beautiful city...

The following paragraphs are excellent examples of a leader sentence followed by clear development of that sentence.

61

H.L. Essay Writing

Moscow is an exceptionally clean city, much cleaner than many in western Europe or America. Even after a sharp fall of snow, the streets are cleared very quickly although little mechanical equipment is available. Most street-sweeping is done by old women in white aprons and black boots, wielding coarse brooms made of twigs. Militiamen posted at hotels, embassies, and public buildings are empowered to make you pick up a cigarette stub, if you toss it on the street instead of in a receptacle, but I never saw this happen.

Moscow is an extraordinarily silent city. Automobile horns are forbidden, and in winter the carpet of snow serves to muffle traffic noises; the trolley buses, operating from overhead wires, are almost soundless, and, since the chief airport is sixteen miles away, aeroplanes are seldom heard directly overhead. Hardly ever in Moscow does anybody hear a loudspeaker, an ambulance siren, a fire engine, or even a police whistle.

Soviet appetite for reading matter is, we should know by now, boundless. There are good bookshops in almost every sizeable town; they are almost always crowded, and a new novel, even if published in a substantial edition will sometimes be sold out on the day it is published. Western authors may well envy this refreshing phenomenon. People have a thirst and enthusiasm for books almost unbelievable by our standards. In the Moscow subway I noticed passengers reading books, not magazines or newspapers, but actual books, while going up or down the escalators.

The guillotine was a neat little device which could separate someone's head from his body in record time. It consisted of a weighted blade with a slanting edge which was guided during its rapid descent by two upright posts. The victim was bound in place and the severed head fell into a basket. This device was extremely popular in revolutionary France and was installed in public view so that no one would miss the operation.

Public transport is one of the nightmares of modern city life. The miserable commuter may stand silent and crushed for up to two hours of every working day. As he battles his way to the exit of train or bus, other human beings become stubborn obstacles in his path. The only emotions he feels are frustration, annoyance and fear that his pocket may be picked in the mad scramble for the doors. This is an inhuman way to travel.

H.L. Essay Writing

Expand the theme in the following "leader sentences" into full paragraphs.

1. I dislike Mondays in Winter......................
2. Fanatics of any kind are dangerous people..........................
3. Did you know that people as they grow older, grow duller?......................
4. The busker gets to know human nature very well......................................
5. The cosmetics industry is founded on lies..
6. Very few people can resist listening to gossip...
7. Many readers today are addicted to gruesome horror fiction.................

The Final Step is Drawing your Essay to a Conclusion

Below are the concluding paragraphs in a debate, in which the speaker was **opposing** the motion that,

In the third world, development is more important than protecting the environment.

... Ladies and gentlemen, it has taken the western world 200 years of destruction and pollution to learn the hard lesson that protecting the environment must be a global priority. In the past 200 years of industrial revolution, we in the west have filled the air we breathe with poison; we have pumped toxic chemicals into rivers, lakes and oceans; we have developed terrifying weapons and devastated large tracts of land in their use. All of this has been done in the name of "development."

Finally in the closing decades of the twentieth century, we have learned the hard way that if we put so-called "development" first then we are systematically destroying the planet we inhabit. Governments now realise that there are votes in the environment issue and that nations now want their environment protected.

And tonight, ladies and gentlemen, you are being asked to consider if, having almost destroyed the western world with misguided industrial development, we should now turn our destructive hands on the Third World. The great giants of the west now promise "development" to the poor and the price is the environment. The truth is, that the west, having poisoned its own territory, is now going to do the same to the poverty-stricken peoples of the undeveloped countries.

H.L. Essay Writing

We, the opposition, say NO! We ask you to throw out this outrageous philosophy. Nothing is more important than the environment. This is especially true in the Third World where short term western greed has already done enough to exploit the poor. The multi-nationals and giant corporations have looked to the undeveloped countries for cheap labour and raw materials. They suppose that in these countries, governments are so anxious for development that they will allow industries which would be opposed in Europe or the U.S.A.

This motion is based on the philosophy of greed. Moreover it is a motion that has already been rejected by the western world. We ask you tonight. Do not impose this terrible philosophy on the peoples of the Third World .... they have suffered enough already.

Do you think the speaker has made a strong argument and a powerful concluding statement? Give reasons for your opinion.

H.L. Essay Writing

Trying out the Structured Approach

Let's take the 1985 essay topic

"International Sport"

and try the planned approach which should result in a well developed, well structured essay.

Step 1 - Brainstorm

Complete the diagram, giving yourself 5-10 minutes to gather ideas.

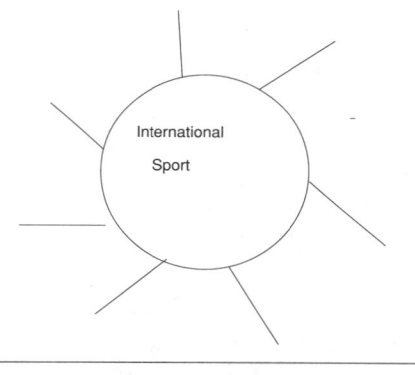

Step 2 — General Introduction

Having thought about the subject, we can now try a draft of an introductory paragraph:

> International sport today is a cut-throat business in which the main aim is to make a lot of money before you retire at the ripe old age of 26. Two generations ago, sport was fun for the enthusiastic amateur who trained in the evenings and at weekends and enjoyed normal life the rest of the time. This person is no longer acceptable at an international level. He or she has been replaced by the fanatical, business-managed professional who drinks carrot juice for breakfast and trains on Christmas Day. International events are now accompanied by a level of media hype and sponsorship unknown in the past. Violence is now part of the international sport scene and huge financial rewards have made for very bitter competition among sportsmen and women.

H.L. Essay Writing

Step 3 — Planning Paragraphs

This is the middle section in your essay in which you develop and argue your ideas in clear, well thought-out paragraphs. Consider the following suggestions to add to your own ideas on the topic:

- politics in sport
- recent news stories
- the excitement generated by international events
- the Olympic Games
- the sports personalities you most admire
- violence
- drug-taking
- very young international competitors.

Step 4 — A Strong Conclusion

If you have explored the subject and thought it through, then the conclusion will follow naturally from what you've written. Look back at the advice given on *Ending Your Essay* in Stage 3.

Now write your essay entitled, *"International Sport."*

Narrative and Dialogue

If you want to write a good narrative and dialogue, then you should study those writers who have developed the craft of telling a good story and dramatising it with excellent dialogue. One such writer is James Herriot. In this extract, he has just tended a favourite horse, and its owner, Mr. Crump, asks him to taste some home-made wine.

I went into the house to wash my hands and Mr. Crump led the way into the kitchen, his big frame lumbering clumsily ahead of me. He proffered soap and towel in his slow-moving way and stood back in silence as I leaned over the long shallow sink of brown earthenware.

As I dried my hands he cleared his throat and spoke hesitantly. "Would you like a drink of ma wine?"

Before I could answer, Mrs. Crump came bustling through from an inner room. She was pulling on her hat and behind her her teenage son and daughter followed, dressed ready to go out.

"Oh Albert, stop it!" she snapped, looking at her husband. "Mr. Herriot doesn't want your wine. I wish you wouldn't pester people so with it!"

The boy grinned. "Dad and his wine, he's always looking for a victim." His sister joined in the general laughter and I had an uncomfortable feeling that Mr. Crump was the odd man out in his home.

"We're going down t'village institute to see a school play, Mr. Herriot," the wife said briskly. "We're late now so we must be off." She hurried away with her children, leaving the big man looking after her sheepishly. There was a silence while I finished drying my hands, then I turned to the farmer. "Well, how about that drink, Mr. Crump?"

He hesitated for a moment and the surprised looked deepened. "Would you.. you'd really like to try some?"

"I'd love to. I haven't had my evening meal yet — I could just do with an aperitif."

"Right, I'll be back in a minute." He disappeared into the large pantry at the end of the kitchen and came back with a bottle of amber liquid and glasses.

"This is ma rhubarb," he said, tipping out two good measures.

I took a sip and then a good swallow, and gasped as the liquid blazed a fiery trail down to my stomach.

"It's strong stuff," I said a little breathlessly, "but the taste is very pleasant. Very pleasant indeed."

Mr. Crump watched approvingly as I took another drink. "Aye, it's just right. Nearly two years old."

I drained the glass and this time the wine didn't burn so much on its way down but seemed to wash around the walls of my empty stomach and send glowing tendrils creeping along my limbs.

"Delicious," I said. "Absolutely delicious."

The farmer expanded visibly. He refilled the glasses and watched with rapt attention as I drank. When we had finished the second glass he jumped to his feet.

"Now for a change I want you to try summat different." He almost trotted to the pantry and produced another bottle, this time of colourless fluid. "Elderflower," he said, panting slightly.

When I tasted it I was amazed at the delicate flavour, the bubbles sparkling and dancing on my tongue.

"Gosh, this is terrific. It's just like champagne. You know, you really have a gift — I never thought home-made wines could taste like this."

Mr. Crump stared at me for a moment and then one corner of his mouth began to twitch and incredibly a shy smile spread slowly over his face. "You're about fust I've heard say that. You'd think I was trying to poison folks when I offer them ma wine — they always shy off but they can sup plenty of beer and whiskey."

"Well they don't know what they're missing, Mr. Crump." I watched while the farmer replenished my glass. "I wouldn't have believed you could make stuff as good as this at home." I sipped appreciatively at the elderflower. It still tasted like champagne.

I hadn't got more than halfway down the glass before Mr. Crump was clattering and clinking inside the pantry again. He emerged with a bottle of contents of a deep blood red. "Try that," he gasped.

I was beginning to feel like a professional taster and rolled the first mouthful around my mouth with eyes half closed. "Mm, mm, yes. Just like an excellent port, but there's something else here — a fruitiness in the background — something familiar about it — it's it's..."

"Blackberry!" shouted Mr. Crump triumphantly, "one of t'best I've done. Made it two back-ends since — it were a right good year for it."

Leaning back in the chair I took another drink of the rich, dark wine; it was round-flavoured, warming, and behind it there was always the elusive hint of the brambles. I could almost see the heavy-hanging clusters of berries glistening black and succulent in the autumn sunshine. The mellowness of the image matched my mood which was becoming more expansive by the minute and I looked round with leisurely appreciation at the rough comfort of the farmhouse kitchen; at the hams and sides of bacon hanging from their hooks in the ceiling, and at my host sitting across the table, watching me eagerly. He was, I noticed for the first time, still wearing his cap.

"You know," I said, holding the glass high and studying its ruby depths against the light. "I can't make up my mind which of your wines I like best. They're all excellent and yet so different."

Mr. Crump, too, had relaxed. He threw back his head and laughed delightedly before hurriedly refilling both of our tumblers. "But you haven't started yet. Ah've got dozens of bottles in there — all different. You must try a few more."

He shambled again over to the pantry and this time when he reappeared he was weighed down by an armful of bottles of differing shapes and colours.

What a charming man he was, I thought. How wrong I had been in my previous assessment of him; it had been so easy to put him down as lumpish and unemotional but as I looked at him now his face was alight with friendship, hospitality, understanding. He had cast off his inhibitions and as he sat down surrounded by the latest batch he began to talk rapidly and fluently about wines and wine making.

Wide-eyed and impassioned he ranged at length over the niceties of fermentation and sedimentation, of flavour and bouquet. He dealt learnedly with the relative merits of Chambertin and Nuits St. George, Montrachet and Chablis. Enthusiasts are appealing but a fanatic is irresistible and I sat spellbound while Mr. Crump pushed endless samples of his craft in front of me, mixing and adjusting expertly.

"How did you find that 'un?"
"Very nice..."
"But sweet, maybe?"
"Well perhaps..."
"Right, try some of this with it." The meticulous addition of a few drops of nameless liquid from the packed rows of bottles. "How's that?"
"Marvellous!"
"Now this 'un. Perhaps a bit sharpish, eh?"
"Possibly... yes..."

Again the tender trickling of a few mysterious droplets into my drink and again the anxious enquiry.
"Is that better?"
"Just right."

The big man drank with me, glass by glass. We tried parsnip and dandelion, cowslip and parsley, clover, gooseberry, beetroot and crab apple. Incredibly, we had some stuff made from turnips which was so exquisite that I insisted on a refill.

Everything gradually slowed down as we sat there. Time slowed down till it was finally meaningless. Mr. Crump and I slowed down and our speech and actions became more and more deliberate. The farmer's visits to the pantry developed into laboured, unsteady affairs; sometimes he took a round-about route to reach the door and on one occasion there was a tremendous crash from within and I feared he had fallen among his bottles. But I couldn't be bothered to get up and see and in due course he reappeared, apparently unharmed.

It was around nine o'clock that I heard the soft knocking on the outer door. I ignored it as I didn't want to interrupt Mr. Crump who was in the middle of a deep exposition. "This," he was saying, leaning close to me and tapping a bulbous flagon with his forefinger. "Thish is, in my 'pinion, comp'rable to a fine Moselle. Made it last year and would 'preciate it if you'd tell me what you think." He bent low over the glass, blinking, heavy-eyed as he poured.
"Now then, wha'd d'you say? Ish or ishn't it?"
I took a gulp and paused for a moment. It all tasted the same now and I had never drunk

H.L. Essay Writing

Moselle anyway, but I nodded and hiccuped solemnly in reply.

The farmer rested a friendly hand on my shoulder and was about to make a further speech when he, too, heard the knocking. He made his way across the floor with some difficulty and opened the door. A young lad was standing there and I heard a few muttered words.
"We 'ave a cow on calving and we phoned surgery and they said vitnery might still be here." Mr. Crump turned to face me. "It's the Bamfords of Holly Bush. They wan' you to go there — jush a mile along t'road."

"Right," I heaved myself to my feet then gripped the table tightly as the familiar objects of the room began to whirl rapidly around me. When they came to rest Mr. Crump appeared to be standing at the head of a fairly steep slope. The kitchen floor had seemed perfectly level when I had come in but now it was all I could do to fight my way up the gradient.

When I reached the door Mr. Crump was staring owlishly into the darkness.
"S'raining," he said. "S'raining like 'ell."

James Herriot
Let Sleeping Vets Lie

1. *Why does the vet accept Mr. Crump's offer of a drink?*
2. *How do the personalities of both characters change as the passage goes on?*
3. *Librarians will tell you that they cannot keep enough copies of James Herriot's books on the shelves.*
   From your reading of this extract, why would you say readers enjoy Herriot's writing?

H.L. Essay Writing

Perhaps the most famous writer of good narrative in English is Charles Dickens. His novels were enormously popular in his own lifetime and are still popular over a hundred years after his death. Why is this so? Unforgettable Characters? Certainly! Spellbinding plots? Yes! But also, a great gift for telling a tale and creating dramatic dialogue. Look at the opening pages of "Great Expectations" and see how the reader is enthralled by the writing from the very beginning.

Chapter 1

My father's family name being Pirrip, and my christian name Philip, my infant tongue could make of both names nothing longer or more explicit than Pip. So I called myself Pip, and came to be called Pip.

I give Pirrip as my father's family name, on the authority of his tombstone and my sister — Mrs. Joe Gargery, who married the blacksmith. As I never saw my father or my mother, and never saw any likeness of either of them (for their days were long before the days of photographs), my first fancies regarding what they were like, were unreasonably derived from their tombstones. The shape of the letters on my father's gave me an odd idea that he was a square, stout, dark man, with curly black hair. From the character and turn of the inscription, "Also Georgiana Wife of the Above," I drew the childish conclusion that my mother was freckled and sickly. To five little stone lozenges, each about a foot and a half long, which were arranged in a neat row beside their grave, and were sacred to the memory of five little brothers of mine — who gave up trying to get a living exceedingly early in that universal struggle — I am indebted for a belief I religiously entertained that they had all been born on their backs with their hands in their trousers-pockets, and had never taken them out in this state of existence.

Ours was marsh country, down by the river, within, as the river wound, twenty miles of the sea. My first most vivid and broad impression of the identity of things, seems to me to have been gained on a memorable raw afternoon towards evening. At such a time I found out for certain, that this bleak place overgrown with nettles was the churchyard; and that Philip Pirrip, late of this parish, and also Georgiana wife of the above, were dead and buried; and that Alexander, Bartholomew, Abraham, Tobias and Roger, infant children of the aforesaid, were also dead and buried; and that the dark flat wilderness beyond the churchyard, intersected with dykes and mounds and gates, with scattered cattle feeding on it, was the marshes; and that the low leaden line beyond was the river; and that the distant savage lair from which the wind was rushing, was the sea; and that the small bundle of shivers growing afraid of it all and beginning to cry, was Pip.

"Hold your noise!" cried a terrible voice, as a man started up from among the graves at the side of the church porch.

"Keep still, you little devil, or I'll cut your throat!"

A fearful man, all in coarse grey, with a great iron on his leg. A man with no hat, and with broken shoes, and with an old rag tied round his head. A man who had been soaked in water, and smothered in mud, and lamed by stones, and cut by flints, and stung by nettles, and torn by briars: who limped and shivered, and glared and growled; and whose teeth chattered in his head as he seized me by the chin.

"O! Don't cut my throat, sir," I pleaded in terror. "Pray don't do it, sir."

"Tell us your name!" said the man. "Quick."

"Pip, sir."

"Once more," said the man, staring at me. "Give it mouth!"

"Pip. Pip, sir."

"Show us where you live," said the man. "Pint out the place!"

I pointed to where the village lay, on the flat in-shore among the alder-trees and pollards, a mile or more from the church.

The man, after looking at me for a moment, turned me upside down, and emptied my pockets. There was nothing in them but a piece of bread. When the church came to itself — for he was so sudden and strong that he made it go head over heels before me, and I saw the steeple under my feet — when the church came to itself, I say, I was seated on a high tombstone, trembling, while he ate the bread ravenously.

"You young dog," said the man, licking his lips, "what fat cheeks you ha' got."

I believe they were fat, though I was at that time undersized for my years, and not strong.

"Darn me if I couldn't eat 'em," said the man, with a threatening shake of his head, "and if I han't half a mind to 't!"

I earnestly expressed my hope that he wouldn't, and held tighter to the tombstone on which he had put me; partly, to keep myself upon it; partly, to keep myself from crying.

"Now lookee here!" said the man. "Where's your mother?"

"There, sir!" said I.

He started, made a short run, and stopped and looked over his shoulder.

"There, sir!" I timidly explained. "Also Georgiana. That's my mother."

"Oh!" said he, coming back. "And is that your father alonger your mother?"

"Yes, sir," said I; "him too; late of this parish."

"Ha!" he muttered then, considering. "Who d'ye live with — supposin' you're kindly let to live, which I han't made up my mind about?"

"My sister, sir — Mrs. Joe Gargery — wife of Joe Gargery, the blacksmith, sir."

"Blacksmith, eh?" said he. And looked down at his leg.

After darkly looking at his leg and at me several times, he came closer to my tombstone, took me by both arms, and tilted me back as far as he could hold me; so that his eyes looked most powerfully down into mine, and mine looked most helplessly up into his.

"Now lookee here," he said, "the question being whether you're to be let live. You know what a file is?"

"Yes, sir."

"And you know what wittles is?"

"Yes, sir."

After each question he tilted me over a little more, so as to give me a greater sense of helplessness and danger.

"You get me a file." He tilted me again. "And you get me wittles." He tilted me again. "You bring 'em both to me." He tilted me again. "Or I'll have your heart and liver out." He tilted me again.

I was dreadfully frightened, and so giddy that I clung to him with both hands and said, "If you would kindly please to let me keep upright, sir, perhaps I shouldn't be sick, and perhaps I could attend more."

He gave me a most tremendous dip and roll, so that the church jumped over its own weather-cock. Then, he held me by the arms in an upright position on the top of the stone, and went on these fearful terms:

"You bring me, to-morrow morning early, that file and them wittles. You bring the lot to me, at that old Battery over yonder.

You do it, and you never dare to say a word or dare to make a sign concerning your having seen such a person as me, or any person sum-ever, and you shall be let to live. You fail, or you go from my words in any partickler, no matter how small it is, and your heart and liver shall be tore out, roasted and ate. Now, I ain't alone, as you may think I am. There's a young man hid with me, in comparison with which young man I am an Angel. That young man hears the words I speak. That young man has a secret way pecooliar to himself, of getting at a boy, and at his heart and at his liver. It is in vain for a boy to attempt to hide himself from that young man. A boy may lock his door, may be warm in bed, may tuck himself up, may draw the clothes over his head, and may think himself comfortable and safe, but that young man will softly creep and creep his way to him and tear him open. I am keeping that young man from harming of you at the present moment, with great difficulty. I find it very hard to hold that young man off of your inside. Now, what do you say?"

I said that I would get him the file, and I would get him what broken bits of food I could, and I would come to him at the Battery, early in the morning.

H.L. Essay Writing

"Say, Lord strike you dead if you don't!" said the man.

I said so and he took me down.

"Now," he pursued, "You remember what you've undertook, and you remember that young man, and you get home!"

"Goo-good night, sir," I faltered.

"Much of that!" said he, glancing about him over the cold wet flat. "I wish I was a frog. Or a eel!"

At the same time, he hugged his shuddering body in both his arms — clasping himself, as if to hold himself together — and limped towards the low church wall. As I saw him go, picking his way among the nettles, and among the brambles that bound the green mounds, he looked in my young eyes as if he were eluding the hands of the dead people stretching up cautiously out of their graves, to get a twist upon his ankle and pull him in.

When he came to the low church wall, he got over it, like a man whose legs were numbed and stiff, and then turned round to look for me. When I saw him turning, I set my face towards home, and made the best use of my legs. But presently I looked over my shoulder and saw him going on again towards the river, still hugging himself in both arms, and picking his way with his sore feet among the great stones dropped into the marshes here and there, for stepping-places when the rains were heavy, or the tide was in.

I looked all round for the horrible young man, and could see no signs of him. But now I was frightened again, and ran home without stopping.

Charles Dickens

From your reading of this narrative, what would you say were **three** of Dickens' most important qualities as a writer? Write a paragraph on **each** of the **three** qualities you select.

Narrative Essay Titles
1. The Connoisseur.
2. Stranger in the Churchyard.

H.L. Essay Writing

Discursive Writing

Many essays demand a well informed writer. Consider for example,

The role of women in Ireland today (1979)

or

The unemployment problem (1983)

You may find that your knowledge of history or economics is very helpful in writing in an informed way. Do you know what is happening in your community? Do you know what issues are affecting the way people vote in elections at present? Do you read or listen to the findings of reports on the state of Irish society today?

The **Combat Poverty Agency** tries to bring public attention to poverty in all its forms in Ireland today. Read the following paragraphs and then write a paragraph of your own entitled:

Women and Poverty in Ireland Today

People have different images of poverty. Some see it as starvation; for others it means being deprived of the things that most people have. Similarly, popular perceptions of the poor vary. For some the poor are malingerers living on the backs of the majority; others view the poor as victims of injustice and inequality.

Your chances of getting on depend very much on the family into which you are born. Therefore, poverty is not the fault of the individual and it is not an accident. All of the evidence for Ireland indicates that poverty is getting worse in that the children of the poor have less and less chance of escaping the lives of poverty led by their parents.

Poverty, then, is not just about a lack of money, as it has been traditionally defined with a male model in mind. It is also about rights and entitlements and the extent to which one is allowed the same access to opportunities and resources as most people. In addition, poverty is about feelings — about how you regard yourself and how others treat you. Being poor often involves feelings of powerlessness, exclusion and being treated as inferior and as lacking in status. These aspects are of major importance for a woman-centred conception of poverty.

Women's poverty is so hidden it is often invisible. There are many ways in which women are undercounted in the poverty statistics.

For instance, many women are not counted as unemployed because it is not worth their while to sign on; or we simply do not know how many of that half of all women (i.e. those working in the home), who are totally dependent on men, get enough money.

Women's poverty is also different because of the emotional difficulties that are often part of it, on top of financial, material and social deprivation. Feelings of guilt, shame and embarrassment are part and parcel of life in poverty for women. The third way in which women's poverty differs is in its origins: sex discrimination is a major cause of female poverty.

It is estimated that up to 20% of people who are currently poor are in the workforce. Many of these are women. Research carried out recently, based on information from 1979, estimated that almost half of all women workers were low paid, 44,000 women workers at that time. We are all familiar with the "cheap" jobs; factory work, shop and supermarket work, waitressing and other jobs in catering, cleaning, hairdressing, etc. — all women's jobs.

Women are lower paid than men because more women work part-time, which is less well-paid than full-time work. Over 70% of part-time workers are women, most of them married. Low pay is not the only disadvantage of these kinds of jobs. Another measure of women's disadvantage in employment is to compare women's wages with those of men. Again, the results are not encouraging. Women in industry now earn only about 60% of the average male weekly wage.

Overall, a conservative estimate is that a minimum of 300,000 women are living in poverty in Ireland. One cannot explain this without reference to concepts like dependency, inequality, and women's exclusion from the opportunity to secure an independent source of income. At the heart of women's poverty is a particular set of beliefs and values that assign women a secondary place in the economy and a primary place in the home. Having full responsibility for childcare and family contributes in no small way to women's poverty.

In the end, it is women who bear the main burden of poverty; it is women who have to manage on totally inadequate incomes, to endure the endless scrimping and saving, and to cope with the debts when the ends simply don't meet. As more men lose their jobs, more women are pushed into a life of poverty, caught in a daily even hourly struggle to keep body and soul together.

Mary Daly, Head of Research **Combat Poverty Agency.**

1. Do you agree with the statements made about poverty in the first three paragraphs of this essay?
2. What are the main points being made in this essay about women's poverty in Ireland?
3. Do you agree with the conclusions Mary Daly comes to in the closing paragraph?
4. What is the essay as a whole aiming to do?

STAGE 5
Writing a Full Essay

Every year, examiners at higher level say that candidates who scored badly on the essay did so because of 3 main factors:

* They did not know how to start their essay.
* They did not know how to organize and paragraph the middle section of their essay.
* They did not know how to successfully conclude their essay.

Look back at what you have learned in the course of using this book.

You have worked on

- Writing clear English
- Writing good opening lines
- Choosing the essay that suits your style
- Gathering ideas
- Developing single paragraphs.

Answer the following questions.
1. Are you reading in order to feed your imagination and intellect? Your essay writing should change and mature over any long period but it will remain dull and unchanging if you have nothing of interest to say or if your vocabulary does not expand to express your ideas.
2. Do you read the letters page in the newspaper to see what people are concerned about and how they express their views?
3. Have you discovered a style of writing that you are best at? When you look at the choice of topics, are you attracted by a certain type of essay? Do you look for descriptive? narrative? discursive? personal? literary subjects?
4. Do you always give time to considering the various possibilities in a title before you put pen to paper?
5. Do you find the 5 minute brainstorm a useful start?

H.L. Essay Writing

Let us take some sample essays of the types we discussed in **Stage 2**. Read through them carefully and choose the one that would suit you.

Mountains	—	descriptive
Reading for pleasure	—	literary
The purpose of education		
Money is the root of all evil		discursive
Emigration is Ireland's greatest single problem	—	Irish interest
The role of the individual in protecting the planet	—	environmental
Why you would or would not like to be a politician in Dáil Eireann.	—	personal

Before you start writing your chosen essay, remember the importance of stages 1-4.

- Observe the basic rules of punctuation and good written English.
- Write good, clear paragraphs, each paragraph developing a single idea.
- Your opening line should be strong and interesting.
- Gather ideas and think about the title before you begin to write the essay.
- It is also a very good idea to look back at the title at frequent intervals as you write. This stops you from wandering off the point. Keep it relevant!
- You are aiming at two or three pages of foolscap. If this is too difficult at this stage, aim for a quality, shorter essay. Don't just fill the pages with words.

H.L. Essay Writing

You are the Examiner

The following essays (pages 78 - 98) are the work of 5th and 6th year students. Put yourself in the position of examiner assessing these essays. Grade them, using the following guidelines:

Content — Are the ideas good? Is the essay thoughtful? Is the candidate a reader? informed? interesting to read?

Expression — Does the candidate show good command of the English language? Is the vocabulary good or very restricted? Are the ideas clearly expressed? Is there any use of imagery or good turn of phrase? Is the style good? Is the essay well paragraphed? Does each paragraph make a point? Are the basic rules of punctuation observed?

Relevance — Is the essay as a whole relevant to the title? Has the candidate obviously looked back frequently to the title in order to keep to the subject?

Now grade each essay and write a short commentary, justifying the grade you gave.

Mountains

Mountains are a rich and varied playground for the enthusiast, a challenge, for the serious mountaineer and a desert for the uninformed. Their inaccessibility, beauty and mystery have inspired awe in men from the beginning of time, and have lured many to a lonely death. Perhaps their greatest attraction is their stubborn immortality. Men die, but the mountains are eternal.

Twentieth century man craves the outdoor life. The human being who lives in a centrally heated cocoon longs for the biting wind and the cloudy mists of the summit. The urban cabbage seeks relief, rediscovery and recreation in the timeless world of the mountain, untouched and unchanging.

The happiest times of my life have been spent in the mountains of Wicklow and Wales. They provided a growing place for my character. They represent freedom and independence from family, school and city restrictions. My original incentive came from my father's interest in scenic beauty and orienteering. He brought me on my first walk in the foothills of the Dublin mountains which I thought at that time was a great and daring adventure.

Mountains are not for those of weak character or mind. Enjoyment is often only gained through endurance and sacrifice. One cannot see the view from the peak without first climbing it. The mountain must be respected, it is rough, harsh and unmerciful. Sunshine at the foot of the mountain can change to blinding rain or dense fog at three thousand feet above sea level. There is no loneliness to equal that of being lost in a fog at the summit. There are no safety nets on a cliff face!

The Welsh mountains have a distinct beauty of their own. They are laced in winter with white streams of rainwater racing down craggy drops, and in summer provide reddish sunrises to greet the early riser.

> I have often heard the expression "Where there's mountains, there's brains" and having met many mountain dwellers I have to agree. People who live on mountains are a different breed. They are welcoming and witty and love conversation with travellers.
>
> People often ask me why I climb and I tell them that it's for pure air and exercise, but the truth is that it goes deeper than that and I find it hard to explain clearly. When I am climbing, I become a different person, more contented and free. The mountains have awakened in me a sense of adventure that would otherwise lie dormant. The mountains are powerful. You must never lose the feeling that they are the masters and you are merely an uninvited traveller in their kingdom.

Re-read the criteria for judging an essay on page 77. (You are the Examiner).

Begin with a rough estimate. Is it outstanding? Very good? Average? Poor? Then focus on particular qualities and your mark can become specific.

Grade the essay.

Write a commentary (mentioning content, expression and relevance) justifying the grade you gave.

Write an essay entitled **Rivers.**

Your mark

$$\frac{?}{100\%}$$

Memories

When my grandmother died last year, she had stopped living in the present and had slipped happily back into her memories. She kept an album of old photographs by her bedside and would show them to any visitor who was prepared to look and listen for an hour. The older the photo was, the more she had to say about it, and she remembered the tiniest details, like where someone had bought the material for the dress she was wearing in 1956 and how much it cost per yard. The strange thing was, she couldn't remember where she had put down her glasses ten minutes ago or whether she had eaten dinner yet.

Memories are like that, you remember what made an impression and forget the boring bits. I can't remember much about my first years in school but I'll never forget the day Margaret Curley's mother came to the classroom door, looking for teacher's blood. I was making a plasticine camel at the moment the door burst open and a strange woman came in roaring. What a disappointment when Miss Mullarkey steered her into the corridor and closed the door firmly behind her. And the thrill of standing on your little chair to try to see out the corridor window! My only vivid childhood memory apart from that is of splitting my head open in the park and getting four stitches on my forehead. I can still smell the antiseptic and it comes back to me every time I walk through hospital doors.

Not everyone has such trivial memories. There are those who would like to blot out their memories of war, hunger and hardship. J.G. Ballard wrote about his memories of internment in Japanese camps in "Empire of the Sun." Others relive their horrors by writing about the camps and ghetto communities of Germany or Eastern Europe. For them, memories are nightmares. When our class visited Russia last year, we went to a cemetery which commemorates the Siege of Leningrad. A million people died there of starvation and cold in the three year siege. I remember people weeping at graves and leaving pieces of food where we would leave flowers. Almost

H.L. Essay Writing

fifty years later, the memories are still powerful and even the tourists walked in silence.

Have you noticed how happier memories have become the publisher's dream? There is a spate of popular books in the shops recalling the childhood of the past. Country childhoods in farmhouse kitchens and city childhoods playing skipping and swinging on lamp posts are making a fortune for those with good memories and the talent to tell a good yarn. If I had kept a diary and written down everything that happened in school, I wouldn't be worrying about the grade I might get in this exam. Just tap out all your little stories on a word processor and watch all the royalties rolling in! Is anyone out there interested in my memories of playdough, finger painting and *Little Rabbit Frou-Frou*?

Something in us needs to remember and recall. New Year's Eve comes and television shows "compilations" of the year's political, sporting and social events and hundreds of little human interest stories. We go on holidays and we snap everything with the camera "in case we forget." We are each of us a little private collection of memories and if my grandmother is anyone to go by, the older we get, the more precious they become..

Consider again the criteria for judging an essay on page 77.

Grade this essay and write a short comment, justifying the grade you gave.

There are many possibilities in this title. Write your own essay entitled ***Memories.***

Your mark
————
100%

Money is the Root of All Evil

Bible-thumping preachers, Salvation Army singers and nuns in quiet cloisters would all proclaim the wickedness of money. But who, I ask you, excluding Gandhi, Buddhist monks and beggars could ever survive without it? The answer is: farmers! People who possess land of their own, home grown comestibles or naturally derived edibles. Here I pause for a brief moment to ask myself the question, "am I a farmer or am I not?" No, I am not a farmer, from which it may logically be deduced that money is an all too necessary commodity for me. And since the drift of world population is from the land to the towns and cities, it is fair to presume that more and more people need legal tender to survive.

In recent weeks, I have been cogitating seriously on the subject of "My aim in this world." My sequence of thought runs like this:

"Why do I go to school?"

"To learn."

"Why do I learn?"

"To become clever and pass examinations."

"Why pass examinations?"

"In order to gain entry to a university."

"Why a university?"

"To learn more and get a degree."

"Why?"

"So I can be employed."

"Why?"

"To work and earn a good salary."

"Why?"

"To have money and therefore have the means of enjoying myself."

This answer, (excuse me if it was long-winded) raises the question of my reason for living. For multitudes of people, the attainment of heavenly glory is their goal, and financial considerations are unimportant. I however live mainly for the present and although I find heaven a very

> attractive concept, I prefer to cross my bridges when I reach them (what other way is possible?).
>
> I also consider that there are far greater evils than the quest for money. There is the desperate desire for power and earthly glory. In living memory, there were tyrants whose mad craving for power drove them to mass murder and enslavement. Money is not at the root of all the evil in this world. The desire for money seems positively innocent and childish when compared with the desire of the megalomaniac for total power.
>
> But this essay is becoming very heavy and serious. Let me come back to myself. I live for the present, for enjoyment, for satisfaction, for pleasure, comfort and happiness. I am neither royal nor aristocratic and so must strive for my goals through money. Therefore I stress emphatically that money is not the root of evil at all, but rather is it the root of a desire to be happy on earth. Now can this be evil?
>
> What then shall I do when I have attained great personal wealth? Quite simply, I shall squander my fortune on frivolous fancies and expensive hobbies, too racy to mention here. I will pursue a life of leisure and pleasure for some to condemn and me to enjoy. Do not be mistaken however, I am neither greedy nor selfish — I believe that everybody should have riches and I most certainly do not want to create a false impression of myself, "Pleasure for all," is my motto, "the more money, the merrier."

Using the criteria given on page 77 — content, expression, relevance — grade this essay and write a short commentary on it.

Write an essay entitled, **Happiness is a Good Bank Account.**

Don't forget the spray diagram if you find this a useful "Brainstorm."

Happiness is a good bank account

Your mark

_____
100%

H.L. Essay Writing

This candidate took a title which could suggest many kinds of essay; descriptive, reflective or narrative. He chose the narrative option.

Roads

They were of different kinds. London's was wet and pot-holed, being pounded at this moment by driving rain. Calcutta's was hard and dry, the clay baking in the noonday sun, particles of dust spreading thinly over open-toed sandals.

School today had been bad, teachers had harassed him, intruded on his solitude. As he relished the feeling he would have on coming home, a spray of muddy water hit him as a London taxi passed on the road. He cursed the driver, but really, nothing mattered much, as he thought of his new "friend."

Professional men usually wear dark, sharply tailored suits, designed to impress the client. Calcutta on a shimmering hot day doesn't call for such sartorial elegance. Casual, light colours are the order of the day. And indeed, this is how we find our man in Calcutta, walking along a road, skirting the noisy crowds and the street vendors.

Our two characters have appointments to keep. For the young consumer, heroin does not grow on trees. London's young man knew this only too well as, coming to the end of the road, he rapped his knuckles on a door. Money passed through the letterbox, goodies came out. Maternal robbery was easy when you had reached that point of desperation where moral considerations no longer counted. She still left cash around in unguarded moments.

The second appointment was different. When three millionaires are negotiating in a comfortable limousine, you feel pity for the London teenager. Our man on that road in Calcutta is far from feeling desperation. But he is merely a link in the chain, a point along a long road from producer to consumer. To the mountains he must go, in search of the raw product. From there his travels may take him to every corner of the globe. From

H.L. Essay Writing

Sydney, New York, San Francisco, London, the roads he travels are paved with gold.

High up the mountain, an old man sits at the door of his mud cabin. His little grandchildren run and play together. In the fields, his sons pick poppies, dreaming of the rich rewards their father will force from the Calcutta businessman.

Pharmacies are always fun... everything neatly packed and labelled in small bottles. London's young man and his friend are quick. In and out, get the goods and party. Between shooting up and mindless swallowing, the world becomes hazy, more distant. Soon, the very idea of reality fades...

Meanwhile, with his consignment, our Eastern friend is passing over France. In recent years, he has acquired a taste for fine wines and spectacular scenery. Travel really does broaden the mind and develop the personality. He muses on the few remaining obstacles before him. His appearance is professional and impeccably respectable. It usually carries him through customs without question. Profits have been good of late and with what he's carrying now, the sky's the limit.

As he delivers his consignment, our young London friend has been in a coma for three days. The hospital ward is desolate, the curtains pale like the victim they shade. Massive drug overdose is a daily reality here. Even the tabloids hardly bother reporting cases unless the victim is the son or daughter of an establishment figure or a celebrity.

The businessman smiles. It's been a good day. The long road was worth it. Prosperity in this life is just a matter of individual effort. Life is for winners.

Grade the essay and comment on it, justifying the grade you gave.

Write your own essay entitled **Roads**.

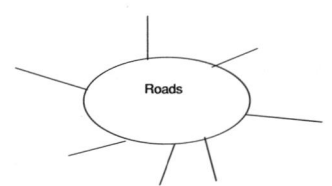

Your mark

100%

My Attitude to Pop Music

My attitude to pop music today is one of disbelief and scepticism. The popular music of today has become a manufactured article which is churned out by executives in skyscraping record company buildings. This is in contrast with the pop music of the 50's and 60's which was fresh, original and above all alive! The music of Buddy Holly and the Beatles was the genuine voice of creative young artists reaching out to other young people. The record companies merely facilitated the artists: they did not control them as they do today.

Pop music is no longer a form of artistic expression, it is a quick way of making a cheap buck. When I listen to my radio, I get quite depressed. Correct me if I'm wrong, but it all sounds the same. This "music" industry reminds me of George Orwell's vision in "1984" of a ministry which wrote songs for the masses.

Music holds a mirror up to society. In the 60's, we had songs of love, war and reconciliation. In the 70's we had "Punks", an aggressive movement. Now, we have a sound which says nothing at all. It is a reflection of our materialistic, self-contained, selfish philosophy. We live in a decadent era and we are drowning in our own flotsam.

Fundamentally, pop music is a form of entertainment. It can however be used to stimulate socio-political awareness. It can rise to heights of great poetry and artistry. There are pieces of popular music that I find very moving. Some people disparage the music of the masses, they believe that only "serious" music has the power to move or stir the imagination. This is not so. Popular music is popular because it touches a chord (!) in people's hearts and appeals to their imaginations. But the artist must have a free hand. Then the music is a celebration of life.

H.L. Essay Writing

> There have been the great scribes of social change. In my opinion, Bob Dylan was a spokesman for an entire generation. The best popular musicians have always been those who wrote and arranged their own material. The songs of Lennon and McCartney have become classics in their own time. The sound of the Rolling Stones was raw and real. Don McClean is a lyricist and poet. Go back even further and you'll find that the popular music of wartime Britain carried people through times of great hardship and reflected emotion in a way that we now find sentimental. But the point is made. Popular music can be a great force in society. It can be history in the making if given free rein. I believe in pop music, and I deplore the financial sham that is masquerading as music on my radio today.

Refer back constantly to the criteria the examiner uses for judging an essay. Avoid being *too* critical of the candidate. Look for the **good points** as well as the bad. You are **judging** not **damning.**

Write an essay entitled, ***The Importance of Music in my Life.***

Your mark

_____
100%

The Role of the Press

The press, for so long master of the business of news, has come under siege in recent years. With the arrival of cable and satellite television and even all-news stations, the press faces stiff competition. But has the role of the press changed and what is the nature of that role in today's world?

The main function of newspapers is to bring news to the general public, to inform us about what is happening at home and abroad. In the past, newspapers were the sole source of news. In the Second World War with military operations on a global scale, the role of the newspaper correspondent was crucial. They were a powerful political force and governments used newspapers to boost the morale of entire nations.

Today, pictures of military conflict are brought by television into our living rooms, almost as the events occur. So what is the role of the newspaper? The printed word can give us in-depth analysis and opinions. Television can make us **see;** newspapers make us **think.** This however can bring its own problems. We talk about "liberal", "left-wing" or "right-wing" newspapers. Instead of reflecting truth, a newspaper editor may offer propaganda. We may be reading, not the editor's beliefs, but those of the paper's wealthy owner. This is an abuse of the printed word. Even the so-called "quality" papers are not above using their editorial columns for personal vendettas in public feuds. Surely the press should not be used for verbal brawls? The public must be informed of scandal, corruption and abuse of power, but always in a responsible, not just a sensation-seeking manner.

The power of the press was most forcefully seen in recent decades in the exposure of the Watergate scandal. Two unknown journalists, brought down one of the most powerful administrations in the world by their work in the "Washington Post." Good journalism is a powerful and necessary force in society.

H.L. Essay Writing

Bad journalism is, unfortunately, a part of the life we live now. As competition increases, standards drop in order to increase readership and profits at any price. The price is integrity which many newspaper journalists and editors seem to have thrown on the scrapheap. Unfortunately, we cannot ignore the British tabloids. Their reputation for sleaze has become legendary and it seems the lower they stoop the higher their profits go. They don't look for news, they look for headlines. It would be funny if it were not so depressing. No public service should sink to their unacceptable level. They breed dirt and they coarsen society. Remember the famous "Gotcha" headline after the sinking of the Belgrano?

Their speciality of course is not political stories but personal news and the more personal the better for readership. They prey upon, torment and harass their victims. They pay vast amounts of money for "inside information," in other words, spying on someone's private life. Ruining careers and lives because of personal indiscretions is not news, nor is it the legitimate function of a newspaper.

A good, free press is an essential element in any democracy. The first step in any dictatorship is to control the press. The journalist is a marked man in a tyranny! In any repressed state the press merely acts as an arm of the state and this is its saddest role and darkest hour.

In the cut-throat world of the media, the press is surviving and holding its own. Our hope must be that high standards will prevail. Newspapers of the future must be thought-provoking, informative, truthful and unprejudiced. These are high ideals — can the press of tomorrow live up to them?

Is this essay interesting? well expressed? relevant?
Grade it and write an essay entitled *Newspapers Today.*

Your mark

100%

H.L. Essay Writing

Write an essay entitled "20 Years from Now."

Many approaches are possible:
- Will you describe the world as you imagine it in 20 years from now?
  — Who will have political power?
  — Will the world as we know it still exist?
  — Will there have been war?
  — Will there be unemployment? famine? disease? more crime...?

- Perhaps you will decide on a more personal approach.
  — How old will you be?
  — What do you hope to have achieved?
  — Where would you like to be living?

- Or you might decide to write about some imaginary character.
  — What kind of life will this person lead?
  — Will he or she be living in a peaceful world?
  — How will technological advances have influenced his or her life?

There are other approaches also if you use your imagination. Your essay could be **Discursive**, **Descriptive** or **Narrative.**

Once you have begun to write essays, you should see the importance of a well structured piece of work. Put another way, this means that your essay should have a clear beginning, middle and end.

- You begin by introducing your topic.

- The main body of your essay is a well paragraphed development of your argument/ideas/narrative.

- You end with a strong concluding paragraph.

Read over the last essay you wrote and ask yourself if it was well structured and paragraphed.

H.L. Essay Writing

The Lure of the Foreign Holiday

The sample essay which follows has a clear beginning, middle and end.

Ireland is a country of spectacular beauty, most often seen through a fine haze of drizzle. When it is not drizzling, it is raining heavily and in winter, it is far worse! The damp Irish soul craves the sunshine and splendour of a foreign holiday. Gone are the days of a week in Mrs. O'Brien's guesthouse in Rathkee (*In* being the important word, since the weather was too foul for any outdoor activities). The pale, freckled Irish face longs for a glowing, even tan.

The lure of the foreign holiday is strongest in January, a month which must be the darkest and dreariest in the calendar. Christmas is over, bills are unpaid and sad faces light up as they pore over glossy brochures with colour photos of the Costapacket. On rush hour buses, weary, sodden commuters turn the pages, gazing at smiling, bronzed beauties and fiery Mediterranean sunsets. Who could resist? "Early booking advisable" shout the tour operators and eager hands reach for their credit cards. Through the driving sleet of February, the cold winds of March and the stubborn frosts of April, the thought of the holiday ahead makes life seem worth while after all.

Structure

Introduction — The holiday scene at home in Ireland.

The travel agents cleverly lure potential holiday-makers at the dullest time of year.

But let us remember that the foreign holiday is a very recent phenomenon. Go back two generations and you'll discover that only the very wealthy travelled abroad. Travel was a different affair then. No hordes of tourists with Olympus OM2s jostling each other for the best angles on the Eiffel Tower. No bunburgers for a quick snack before the bus zooms 200 miles to the next town on our itinerary. No disco music blaring out this year's holiday tune on polluted beaches. Travel in the past was for the very privileged few. It was Thomas Cook who invented the "package deal" a hundred years ago and so began a world-wide phenomenon that eventually brought travel to the masses.

History and growth of the foreign holiday

It is a sad fact that this form of holiday now lures too many people for comfort. Every August brings television pictures of tiny tots sitting plaintively on dad's suitcase while the intercom announces "further delays due to the French air controllers' strike!" The skyways are jammed and airports have become mini cities catering to thousands of disillusioned holidaymakers. The curled up ham sandwich and plastic cup of coffee gets more unappetizing with each passing minute.

Disadvantages of the popular "Package Holiday"

The "sophisticated" traveller now bypasses the popular sunspots. Instead he heads for ski or adventure holidays at off-peak times (becoming more difficult to find). The travel agent lures affluent clients to white sandy beaches in more exotic destinations in the West Indies or the Caribbean. Sunday magazines now carry tempting pictures of "faraway hideaways and luxurious, exotic resorts." These are attractive and alluring, simply because they are exclusive. They deliberately exclude Mr. and Mrs. Ordinary and their splashing toddlers at the hotel pool. Those who have tasted the Bahamas, are unlikely to return to Benidorm.

Dodging the crowds .... foreign holidays with a difference for the more adventurous

For many people, the best part of their foreign holiday is bragging about it afterwards. They despise "beach holidays" of any kind. For them, "island hopping" in Greece is a massive waste of time. These people are to be found cruising on the Upper Nile or sightseeing on the Lower Volga. They talk nonchalantly about nightlife n Istanbul, wonderful markets in Mombasa, touring in Sri Lanka and pony-trekking in Peru. Not for them the tower block hotels favoured by the "pile 'em high, sell 'em cheap" travel companies. The well-heeled are constantly looking for unchartered destinations. These up-market holidaymakers criss-cross the globe in an effort to find what no one else has yet experienced.

Snobbery and the foreign holiday ..... the wealthy traveller enjoys more exciting and exclusive destinations.

H.L. Essay Writing

And what is it all for? Do we travel to broaden the mind? to show off to our neighbours? to see if life is better elsewhere? to break the monotony of dull, working lives? The answer must be that, like Columbus, we travel to satisfy a spirit of curiosity and adventure. Like little children who stray from their parents, we want to see what is over the hill or around the corner. For most of us, it is two weeks in the year in which we live, eat, and see things differently. Who can argue with that?

Conclusion — some general considerations on the ure of the foreign holiday.

Write an essay entitled, **The Appeal of Television.**

Your mark

100%

The following essay on

The Purpose of Education

was written by a 6th year student who structured it very well. Notice that his introductory paragraph is very strong and serious and he then shows that he is capable of writing a more light-hearted style in paragraph 2. Notice also that each paragraph has a strong opening sentence in which he makes a clear statement. The rest of the paragraph then develops and argues that point.

Read the essay, paragraph by paragraph, noting in the right hand column the main point made in each paragraph.

Structure

The foundation of all civilised life is education. In modern society, we have made it a right rather than a privilege, and this must be seen as one of the greatest achievements of the past century.

(What is the main point in each paragraph?)

Introduction

This does not however mean that every recipient of compulsory education is grateful. Gone are the days of angelic, smiling faces in unblemished uniform and dazzling shoes, of marbles and conkers and "talk-and-incur-the-wrath-of-the-most-supreme" attitude. All this has been replaced by aggressive dressing and the mafia-style "you hitta us, we hitta you" teacher-pupil relationship. Education is influenced by the outside world. Factors such as unemployment, poor housing and lawless communities affect the pupil population. Education sways with the tide of society, so to speak.

....

Our concern however is the purpose of education. I believe that it should instill in the mind a library of ideas, beliefs and attitudes. When we need to ponder a problem or discuss any topic, we then have a mind full of resources. As we furnish a house with chairs,, beds, and modern conveniences, so we furnish the mind with ideas. There are many examples of people who fulfilled their life's ambitions and attained great status without education, but let it be remembered that these were exceptional people who succeeded in spite of this lack, and not because of it.

Education is beneficial in our social lives. With it, we can stand on our own two feet and not take a back seat to anyone. We can argue a case reasonably but firmly, and feel confident in any situation. A good vocabulary will never go amiss on a social evening or on a formal occasion. And the educated person will be open to the views of others and be tolerant of opinions which differ from his own. Education should break down the barriers created by prejudice and ignorance.

It should also make a disciplined individual with the willpower to stick with any task, no matter how tedious or demanding. For the Leaving Certificate student it is a matter of sitting at the desk at night, taking out the books, and forgetting about the television or any other distraction. It is a silent religion. The potential doctor or barrister must be single-minded. It is not possible to explore the argument of a Shakespearean sonnet while listening to the music of the 1990s. It takes a lot of grit to sit and study for four hours a night, but with regular practice, it gets to be as routine as breakfast every morning or sleep at night. It also develops a strong character that will stand to you later in life.

....

Education also helps us develop a working relationship with authority. The teacher is not a malicious brute whose sole intention is to see us out of a job and out of luck for the rest of our lives. Good educational institutions manage to create an atmosphere of co-operation and goodwill between teachers and taught. There is little point in having a well developed brain if you cannot get on with others or have never developed a sense of humour. Education is not only for the intellect, it should produce a well balanced human being who has something to offer society.

....

H.L. Essay Writing

Overall, I think the purpose of education is to make every person as good and as happy as he or she can be, and to go some way towards creating an equal society. When Captain Boyle in O'Casey's "Juno and the Paycock" says, "What is the stars?" we all laugh at his comical ignorance, but none of us aspires to be like him.

Conclusion

What grade would you give this essay? Justify the grade.

Write an essay entitled, **Schools Today**.

Your mark

_____
100%

H.L. Essay Writing

The following newspaper article was written by Frank Mac Donald, environment correspondent for the *Irish Times*. Examine the structure of the article and briefly state what main point is being emphasised in each paragraph.

Mass Madness on Wheels

Nothing has changed the way we live more than the car. It has made all sorts of things possible, from one-stop shopping to bungalows in the countryside. It is the grand prize in almost every TV game show and charity draw; you can even win one for paying your ESB bill on time.

....

Cars offer something uniquely exclusive — a personalised form of transport, cocooned from the great unwashed, where you can shave, listen to the radio and do your business by telephone, all on the way into work. No wonder the most sought-after "perk" is a company car — preferably with a free petrol pump to "fill her up."

....

Time magazine proudly proclaimed in a recent advertisement that its readers owned 38 million cars and if all of these cars were stretched bumper to bumper they would circle the equator 4,5 times.

....

Worldwide, there are about 400 million vehicles on the road, with a record 126,000 new cars rolling off assembly lines every working day.

....

Opinion polls which ask people who haven't got a car whether they would like one usually get a resounding "yes," because the car is undoubtedly the most desired object in human history. But if you ask people whether they would like to live in the sort of dirty, dangerous, socially-polarised, fume-filled greenhouse that would result if everyone's wish to own a car were granted, you would get a different answer.

....

Instead of facilitating individual mobility, the proliferation of automobiles has bred a crisis of its own — congestion. The M25 "orbital motorway" on the outskirts of London was supposed to provide a quick route around the city. But as soon as it was completed, the road was clogged with cars, proving the point that traffic always expands to fill the space available to it.

....

99

H.L. Essay Writing

The Worldwatch Institute calculates that at least a third of an average city's land is devoted to catering for cars, if you count all the roads, parking lots, garages, petrol stations and other elements of the "automobile infrastructure." In Dublin, hundreds of buildings have been pulled down over the past 20 years to make the city swallow the traffic pouring into it. And as the number of car-borne commuters increases steadily year by year, the centre is turning into a huge surface car park — most of it illegal.

Cars also exact a frightening toll in human life. An estimated quarter-of-a-million people are killed in traffic accidents around the world every year, with millions more suffering injuries. An average of over 400 people are killed annually in traffic accidents on Irish roads and nearly 8,000 more are injured. That is someone else's department.

When it comes to pollution, cars are hard to beat — As the Worldwatch Institute points out, cars, trucks and buses play a prominent role in generating virtually all the major air pollutants, especially in cities.

The day is not far off when private cars will have to be banned from city centres. Anyone who thinks about it for more than half-a-minute will accept that we cannot go on as we are, plundering the earth for a system of transport that grows more inequitable and less efficient the harder we try to make it work.

Yet our own government seems determined to continue making the same old mistakes, egged on by a powerful roads lobby. In its EC-funded National Development Plan, the government has allocated almost £1,000 million for roads and just £45 million for public transport.

Meanwhile, a London-Irish developer seems to have secured powerful political support for his plans to build a 1.5 million square-foot shopping centre in Palmerstown, on a 200-acre site strategically located at the junction of the Western By-pass motorway and the Galway Road — even though there is no provision for it in the Dublin County Development Plan. The car park alone would occupy 50 acres of land and there would be enough space there to accommodate up to 10,000 cars. Will we never learn?

Frank MacDonald

Now write your own essay entitled, ***The Tyranny of the Private Car.***

H.L. Essay Writing

There are times when you feel uninspired and unable to write. At such times, it is a good idea to read someone else's ideas on a subject to give yourself something to agree with or react to. The following pages do just that.

Only a madman would choose to live in a modern city

"Avoid the rush-hour" must be the slogan of large cities the world over. If it is, it's a slogan no one takes the least notice of. Twice a day, with predictable regularity, the pot boils over. Wherever you look it's people, people, people. The trains which leave or arrive every few minutes are packed: an endless procession of human sardine tins. The streets are so crowded, there is hardly room to move on the pavements. The queues for buses reach staggering proportions. It takes ages for a bus to get to you because the traffic on the roads has virtually come to a standstill. Even when a bus does at last arrive, it's so full, it can't take any more passengers. This whole crazy system of commuting stretches man's resources to the utmost. The smallest unforeseen event can bring about conditions of utter chaos. A power-cut, for instance, an exceptionally heavy snowfall or a minor derailment must always make city-dwellers realise how precarious the balance is. The extraordinary thing is not that people put up with these conditions, but that they actually choose them in preference to anything else.

Large modern cities are too big to control. They impose their own living conditions on the people who inhabit them. City-dwellers are obliged by their environment to adopt a wholly unnatural way of life. They lose touch with the land and rhythm of nature. It is possible to live such an air-conditioned existence in a large city that you are barely conscious of the seasons. A few flowers in a public park (if you have the time to visit it) may remind you that it is spring or summer. A few leaves clinging to the pavement may remind you that it is autumn. Beyond that, what is going on in nature seems totally irrelevant. All the simple, good things of life like sunshine and fresh air are at a premium. Tall buildings blot out the sun. Traffic fumes pollute the atmosphere. Even the distinction between day and night is lost. The flow of traffic goes on unceasingly and the noise never stops.

The funny thing about it all is that you pay dearly for the "privilege" of living in a city. The demand for accommodation is so great that it is often impossible for ordinary people to buy a house of their own. Exorbitant rents must be paid for tiny flats which even country hens would disdain to live in. Accommodation apart, the cost of living is very high. Just about everything you buy is likely to be more expensive than it would be in the country.

In addition to all this, city-dwellers live under constant threat. The crime rate in most cities is very high. Houses are burgled with alarming frequency. Cities breed crime and violence and are full of places you would be afraid to visit at night. If you think about it, they're not really fit to live in at all. Can anyone really doubt that the country is what man was born for and where he truly belongs?

Write an essay entitled, **Modern City Life.**

101

H.L. Essay Writing

New fashions in clothing are created solely for the commercial exploitation of women

Whenever you see an old film, even one made as little as ten years ago, you cannot help being struck by the appearance of the women taking part. Their hair-styles and make-up look dated; their skirts look either too long or too short; their general appearance is, in fact, slightly ludicrous. The men taking part in the film, on the other hand, are clearly recognizable. There is nothing about their appearance to suggest that they belong to an entirely different age.

This illusion is created by changing fashions. Over the years, the great majority of men have successfully resisted all attempts to make them change their style of dress. The same cannot be said for women. Each year a few so-called "top-designers" in Paris or London lay down the law and women the whole world over rush to obey. The decrees of the designers are unpredictable and dictatorial. This year, they decide in their arbitrary fashion, skirts will be short and waists will be high, zips are in and buttons are out. Next year the law is reversed and far from taking exception no one is even mildly surprised.

If women are mercilessly exploited year after year, they have only themselves to blame. because they shudder at the thought of being seen in public in clothes that are out of fashion, they are annually blackmailed by the designers and the big stores. Clothes which have been worn only a few times have to be discarded because of the dictates of fashion. When you come to think of it, only a woman is capable of standing in front of a wardrobe packed full of clothes and announcing sadly that she has nothing to wear.

Changing fashions are nothing more than the deliberate creation of waste. Many women squander vast sums of money each year to replace clothes that have hardly been worn. Women who cannot afford to discard clothing in this way, waste hours of their time altering the dresses they have. Hem-lines are taken up or let down; waist-lines are taken in or let out; neck-lines are lowered or raised, and so on.

No one can claim that the fashion industry contributes anything really important to society. Fashion designers are rarely concerned with vital things like warmth, comfort and durability. They are only interested in outward appearance and they take advantage of the fact that women will put up with any amount of discomfort, providing they look right. There can hardly be a man who hasn't at some time in his life smiled at the sight of a woman shivering in a flimsy dress on a wintry day, or delicately picking her way through deep snow in dainty shoes.

When comparing men and women in the matter of fashion, the conclusions to be drawn are obvious. Do the constantly changing fashions of women's clothes, one wonders, reflect basic qualities of fickleness and instability? Men are too sensible to let themselves be bullied by fashion designers. Do their unchanging styles of dress reflect basic qualities of stability and reliability? That is for you to decide.

What is your reaction to the opinions expressed here?

Write an essay entitled, **Women and Fashion.**

Childhood is certainly not the happiest time of your life

It's about time somebody exploded that hoary old myth about childhood being the happiest period of your life. Childhood may certainly be fairly happy, but its greatest moments can't compare with the sheer joy of being an adult. Who ever asked a six-year-old for an opinion? Children don't have opinions, or if they do, nobody notices. Adults choose the clothes their children will wear, the books they will read and the friends they will play with. Mother and father are kindly but absolute dictators. This is an adult world and though children may be deeply loved, they have to be manipulated so as not to interfere too seriously with the lives of their elders and betters. The essential difference between manhood and childhood is the same as the difference between independence and subjection.

For all the nostalgic remarks you hear, which adult would honestly change places with a child? Think of the years at school: the years spent living in constant fear of examinations and school reports. Every movement you make, every thought you think is observed by some critical adult who may draw unflattering conclusions about your character. Think of the curfews, the martial law, the times you had to go to bed early, do as you were told, eat disgusting stuff that was supposed to be good for you. Remember how "gentle" pressure was applied with remarks like "if you don't do as I say, I'll.." and a dire warning would follow.

Even so, these are only part of a child's troubles. No matter how kind and loving adults may be, children often suffer from terrible, illogical fears which are the result of ignorance and an inability to understand the world around them. Nothing can equal that abject fear a child may feel in the dark, the absolute horror of childish nightmares. Adults can share their fears with other adults; children invariably face their fears alone. But the most painful part of childhood is the period when you begin to emerge from it: adolescence. Teenagers may rebel violently against parental authority, but this causes them great unhappiness. There is a complete lack of self-confidence during this time. Adolescents are over-conscious of their appearance and the impression they make on others. They feel shy, awkward and clumsy. Feelings are intense and hearts easily broken. Teenagers experience moments of tremendous elation or black despair. And through this turmoil, adults seem to be more hostile than ever.

What a relief it is to grow up. Suddenly you regain your balance; the world opens up before you. You are free to choose; you have your own place to live in and your own money to spend. You do not have to seek constant approval for everything you do. You are no longer teased, punished or ridiculed by heartless adults because you failed to come up to some theoretical standard. And if on occasion you are teased, you know how to deal with it. You can simply tell other adults to go to hell: you are one yourself.

Write an essay entitled *Growing Up*.

H.L. Essay Writing

Television is doing irreparable harm

"Yes, but what did we do before there was television?" How often we hear statements like this! Television hasn't been with us all that long, but we are already beginning to forget what the world was like without it. Before we admitted the one-eyed monster into our homes, we never found it difficult to occupy our spare time. We used to enjoy civilised pleasures. For instance, we used to have hobbies, we used to entertain our friends and be entertained by them, we used to go outside for our amusements to theatres, cinemas, restaurants and sporting events. We even used to read books and listen to music and broadcast talks occasionally. All that belongs to the past. Now all our free time is regulated by the "goggle-box." We rush home or gulp down our meals to be in time for this or that programme. We have even given up sitting at table and having a leisurely evening meal, exchanging the news of the day. A sandwich and a glass of beer will do — anything, providing it doesn't interfere with the programme. The monster demands and obtains absolute silence and attention. If any member of the family dares to open his mouth during a programme, he is quickly silenced.

Whole generations are growing up addicted to the telly. Food is left uneaten, homework undone, and sleep is lost. The telly is a universal pacifier. It is now standard practice for mother to keep the children quiet by putting them in the living-room and turning on the set. It doesn't matter that the children will watch rubbishy commercials or spectacles of sadism and violence — so long as they are quiet.

There is a limit to the amount of creative talent available in the world. Every day, television consumes vast quantities of creative work. That is why most of the programmes are so bad: it is impossible to keep pace with the demand and maintain high standards as well. When millions watch the same programmes, the whole world becomes a village, and society is reduced to the conditions which obtain in pre-literate communities. We become utterly dependent on the two most primitive media of communication: pictures and the spoken word.

Television encourages passive enjoyment. We become content with second-hand experiences. It is so easy to sit in our armchairs watching others working. Little by little, television cuts us off from the real world. We get so lazy, we choose to spend a fine day in semi-darkness, glued to our sets, rather than go out into the world itself. Television may be a splendid medium of communication, but it prevents us from communicating with each other. We only become aware how totally irrelevant television is to real living when we spend a holiday by the sea or in the mountains, far away from civilisation. In quiet, natural surroundings, we quickly discover how little we miss the hypnotic tyranny of King Telly.

Write an essay entitled *The Tyranny of Television.*

Practical Details

When writing an essay for class:
1. Write the essay title, then leave a line before beginning the essay itself.
2. Leave a good margin on the left side of the page (wide enough for your teacher to insert corrections.)
3. Write clearly. It's a good test to ask someone you know to read your handwriting. Do you write too big or too small? Do you lean too heavily on the pen? Is a ballpoint pen making you write too fast and carelessly?
4. Be sure to paragraph your work, and don't forget punctuation and inverted commas.
5. Buy a pocket dictionary so you can easily check spellings before you write them down.
6. Read your essay aloud to yourself before you hand it in. It's the very best way to check for errors.

When writing in the exam:
1. Have everything you need to hand — ruler, red biro, good pen, and spare pen.
2. Choose your essay carefully and then stick to the one you choose.
3. Don't start writing the essay immediately. Time spent planning is valuable time. There are no marks for finishing before the other candidates. The essay carries more marks than any other single question so give it your very best efforts.
4. Stop writing every so often and read back over what you have written. This helps to keep your essay unified. Also, look back at the title to be sure you're keeping the essay relevant.
5. At the end, don't just come to a halt; come to a conclusion. The last paragraph should be as strong and impressive as the first. Give it time and round off your writing so that the examiner feels s/he has read something very complete and satisfying.